DIVORCE HURTS:

He Doesn't Want Me to be His Wife Anymore

(Steps to help heal the hurt and pain associated with divorce)

by

DANA MOBLEY-HAMMETT

Scripture quotations identified "NIV" are taken from the *Holy Bible, New International Version®, NIV®*, Copyright ©1973, 1978, 1984 by International Bible Society. Used by permission of Zondervan. All rights reserved.

Scripture quotations identified "NKJV" are taken from the New King James Version. Copyright ©1982 by Thomas Nelson, Inc. Used with permission. All rights reserved.

Divorce Hurts: He Doesn't Want Me to be His Wife Anymore
ISBN: 978-0-88144-014-0
Copyright © 2010 by Dana Mobley- Hammett

Published by
Thorncrown Publishing
A Division of Yorkshire Publishing Group
9731 East 54th Street
Tulsa, OK 74146
www.yorkshirepublishing.com

Printed in the United States of America. All rights reserved under International Copyright Law.
Cover and/ or contents may not be reproduced in any manner with out the express written consent of the author.

Dedication

This book is dedicated with love to all the hurting women who have dealt with a painful separation and/or divorce.

To my son (Ray) and daughter (Danielle), whom I love dearly who also experienced the hurt and pain of a family being destroyed and torn apart through a divorce. I thank God for blessing me with both of you.

My prayer is that God will use my story and the testimony of the women featured in this book *to help heal the hurt and pain from the broken-hearted, especially the many members of the Body of Christ that the enemy came to destroy their marriages too...but the Lord will ALWAYS have the last word, just as Jesus did the day he died on the cross...and so it is done.*

> **The thief does not come except to steal, and to kill, and to destroy. I have come that they may have life, and that they may have it more abundantly.**
>
> **(John 10:10 NIV)**

CONTENTS

INTRODUCTION 6

FOREWORD 10

CHAPTER 1:
    Love & Marriage 11

CHAPTER 2:
    Marriage Built on Insecurities 30

CHAPTER 3:
    Issues of Marriage 43

CHAPTER 4:
    Dealing with Guilt 55

CHAPTER 5:
    Feelings of No Respect 71

CHAPTER 6:
    Getting Another Chance 80

CHAPTER 7:
    Divorce Hurts 92

CHAPTER 8:
    Grief Stages 105

CHAPTER 9:
    Restoration & Healing 117

CHAPTER 10:
   Deliverance from Troubles 127

CHAPTER 11:
   Finding Joy, Peace, & Happiness 134

CHAPTER 12:
   It's a New Day 143

Conclusion 160

For More Information 162

Scriptures for Healing 163

Acknowledgments 165

Bibliography 167

INTRODUCTION

I wanted to share my real life experience as a woman dealing with the hurt and pain of divorce. This book is not intended to hurt anyone and, for the record, was not written to cause division or animosity toward anyone. This is my story, my view, and my truth of what happened in the beginning, the middle, and the end of my marriage. I will not reveal the name of my ex-husband. It's really not important. What is important to me is helping others heal from the hurt of dealing with such a painful experience via the chapters of my life.

At times I find myself wondering what it all meant and how worthwhile my marriage was. And I ask, "But what have I done?" The reality is that divorce happens, and your dreams of "forever" are shattered by situations and circumstances that are not in your control.

Now I am divorced after twenty-two years of marriage. I finally realized, after the fact, how much "Divorce Hurts." It has taken quite some time for me to get over the shock and disbelief that the man I had loved since my youth no longer wanted me to be his wife anymore. I had to accept him moving on.

My book is about the effects of suffering from a case of distrust, insecurities, blame, shame, rejection, and loneliness. Why? Because the man I've loved all these years and believed loved me unconditionally would never

Divorce Hurts: He Doesn't Want Me as His Wife Anymore

leave me nor forsake me. This is about how I was not a perfect wife. Yet, I gave the best of myself the only way I knew how; through being devoted, working hard, and giving unconditional love to my husband.

Now I'm alone, disappointed, frustrated, and shocked that my ex-husband would follow through with a divorce, hurt me, and not want me to be his wife. I feel he left me and didn't even appreciate all the sacrifices, contributions, and support that I had for our family—the years and history between us and even the pressure of being "his" wife. I recall how he treated me with such disregard after his leaving, and his words were so cold, without feeling or emotion. One of his favorite sayings during our divorce process which I will never forget until the day I die is: "It's all about me and my feelings."

I'm thinking not only does he disregard me, but his words seemed to have no regard for our children either. As I look in my son's and daughter's eyes, I can see the disappointment, hurt, and pain that they also are experiencing. But, as their mother, there is nothing I can do to change the situation. I felt so helpless in being unable to ease their hurt. So, this is how our family and the marriage ends—feeling like a huge failure, which I can compare to brutal death with no hope of ever being together again.

When I was just at the point of depression taking hold of me and making me want to give up on myself, I found a mature love and romance in my God and Savior, Jesus Christ, who strengthens me daily through His word. When I was alone, weeping and crying until I made myself sick, I felt like I had no one. I prayed to God to show me in His word why I didn't have a husband to love me unconditionally, to love me just for me, for who I was, and to lay down his entire life for me. God, in his loving compassion, did show me:

> *For your Maker is your husband - the Lord Almighty is His name - the One of Israel is your Redeemer; He is called the God of all the earth.*
>
> **(Isaiah 54:5 NIV)**

Afterwards, I found the comfort, assurance, and protection of my Father up above. HIS unconditional love will last a lifetime, and I know I'm safe in His care.

Finally, *Divorce Hurts: He Does Not Want Me To Be His Wife Anymore*, explains how I accepted that my marriage was over. Finding peace and joy that only God can supply, I understand that God takes us through storms of life to make us stronger. God witnessed what happened to my marriage, and through HIS grace and mercy I made it through the hurt and pain of rejection and feeling like a failure at marriage and as a wife. I will explain how my divorce has brought me wisdom, courage, patience, and growth to move on in hopes of a brighter future to begin a new chapter of my life. God has also shown me, and I do believe:

> **And we know that all things work together for good to those who love God, to those who are called according to His purpose.**
>
> **(Romans 8:28 NKJV)**

This is my testimony of how good God has been to me, and I hope and pray that this book will help heal the hurt and pain associated with divorce not only for women, but their children, family, and friends because divorce may have hurt someone in your life too.

FOREWORD

Testimony

If you are a woman reading this book, it probably means the unimaginable just happened in your life. Your best friend is gone. The person who was supposed to stay by your side for better or worse, for richer or poorer, through sickness and in health is no longer there.

I know exactly how you feel because that happened to me. My husband and I had been married fourteen years when he decided he didn't want to be married anymore.

Shortly after my husband left, a minister told me to "trust in God." I thought that meant trust in God to bring my husband back home, but now, five years later, I know it meant trust in God to do the right things in my life. It meant trust in God to take care of me like nobody else can; trust in God to restore me.

You will experience all sorts of emotions throughout this journey, but please remember to trust in God, draw closer to Him, and pray for His will to be done in your life.

I know it's hard to believe, but the pain will go away, you will laugh again, and you will look forward to the future again. Surround yourself with people who will pray for you and with you and "trust in God."

God bless,
Freda

CHAPTER 1
Love and Marriage

All things have a beginning, and so it is with *Divorce Hurts*. It is of paramount importance for you to think long and hard on how you first met the man who would one day become your husband. This process of "appropriate interpolation" (curing) is necessary to heal the hurt and pain associated with divorce.

Call the healing process "a sifting," or call it what you want—but write down your feelings. Study it. Think about it. Think about what made you want to be with this man in the first place, what made him the guy of your choice. Remember the good times and how your interest in him grew until you both wanted to call each other daily, see each other as often as possible. This was the courtship time, and it blossomed into something special. He became the guy you would call your very own.

When going through a difficult situation, it is very beneficial to write your thoughts and feelings down on paper. While thinking back on your relationship, you might remember something that at the time should have been a "red flag" warning, telling you this might not really be the right person for you.

Sometimes we get so caught up in our "feelings" that we focus on wanting to be loved so much that we ignore certain dysfunctional signs. When meeting an attractive person who shows us attention and affection, it is very easy to get caught up in our emotions and not think straight. That situation can lead us to erroneously assume this must be the "right" person to love us. Sadly, this is not always the case.

In order to better determine the validity of your attraction, it is very important to spend time with that one person in different situations and atmospheres. During these times, it would be wise to pay close attention to their habits. Keep a clear mind. Don't ignore any warning signs, no matter how small or seemingly insignificant. At the beginning of a new relationship, when something happens to cause you to pause, it is all too easy to either ignore it or tell yourself it was just a mistake that everything will be okay.

Especially if he asks for forgiveness, we too often hurriedly assure ourselves that everything will be okay, ignoring the warning sign. This doesn't mean we shouldn't forgive. Just keep the eyes and mind alert, not letting emotions and feelings cloud our judgment. In this way we are alert to our senses, heeding warnings in case the situation is not healthy.

Don't allow yourself to be overwhelmed by insecurity. Many times an insecure person will fall into the thinking trap in which she feels this is the only person who will make her happy or love her, or no one else will come along. There is an old saying that says in part: True love will never fail, and the relationship will be able to weather the storms of a lifetime if it is truly meant to be.

Life is full of choices—some good and some bad. The good thing is that we sometimes get another chance to find out what we want and need from a relationship.

> **Love must be sincere.**
>
> **(Romans 12:9 NIV)**

Before we go looking for love, it is extremely important we learn to know and love ourselves. The best way to do this is spend time alone; learn to love and accept you. Be true to yourself and accept who you are…just for who you are. Don't look at others as we all have had different experiences and come from different backgrounds. Therefore, don't expect to think, act, and even behave like the person next to you.

It is a fact that by the time a child is five to six years of age, their morals and values are pretty much instilled, as well as a set part of their makeup unless a dramatic event happens that alters his or her life in a major way.

Now, having waxed philosophical, I invite you to take a journey with me as I look back at my life, observing how my ex-husband and I met and the relationship evolved.

In looking back I have tried to be honest in identifying the problem areas that should have warned me to keep on moving. Though I recognized several red flags/warning signs back at the beginning of the relationship, like so many others caught up in the feelings and emotions of the moment, subconsciously I must have figured, hoped, or prayed that somehow my love could get him to change. After all, isn't that the right thing to do for a person you believe in and truly love?

It all began just before my freshman year of high school. With nothing to do, my girlfriends and I had ended up at the football stadium, just hanging out, and looking for something to do. Fortunately for us, the boys were having football practice that day. I don't recall the time of day, but I do recall the first time I laid eyes on my future husband.

When the team was practicing at the football stadium, my friends and I looked up at the entrance—there he stood, a tall, good looking, nicely built young man. I remember thinking to myself, *Wow!* Out loud I asked, "Who is that?"

One of my girlfriends answered, "That's the new guy. He'll be going to school here this year."

Oh great...my dreams had come true. I remember consciously thinking: *That's going to be my boyfriend.* Not only was I young and naive, I didn't have much self-confidence or experience, especially when it came to guys. To be honest, before then, I never really looked at a boy with such immediate adoration. I kept thinking: *This must be love at first sight!*

In reality it was months before I saw him again and hadn't really given him much thought since that day at the stadium.

Divorce Hurts: He Doesn't Want Me as His Wife Anymore

How it happened was my older brother was going to a party this particular night at the small town club hangout. Having nothing to do, I asked to go with him. It was not unusual for me to hang out with him because my mom worked all the time, and my dad was usually doing his thing at the town bars.

So there I was, at the club. Shortly after arriving, I met up with my friends and was just visiting when the young man of my dreams came up and asked me to dance. I couldn't believe it! Out of all the girls in the club that night, he asked me to dance. Right then and there I knew he was the one for me.

After that evening this young man pursued me for months, insisting all he wanted was for me to be his girlfriend. I was smart, played it cool, and didn't give in too soon or too easily. He kept after me because I was "different" from the other girls he had dated.

The saying, "Love is blind," is so true. It took me a while to find out this guy's past and present. It turns out my dream guy was a big flirt and had a great instinct on how to be a player. Since an early age he had been sexually active. In fact, while starting a relationship with me, he already had an older girlfriend and was more than willing to drop her for me. I heard she left town for certain reasons I will not mention. However, it had all been a mistake, their relationship was over, and he didn't want to be with her any more. Lost in love or lust, I believed him at the time.

No one could tell me anything bad about him. I wouldn't listen, for in my eyes he could do no wrong. When we were together, he made me feel like a princess, and like I was the only girl in the world he wanted.

Since he lived in town, and I lived in the country, it was easy for me not to know what was going on behind my back. Later on, I realized his words were deceitful, and he had lied and cheated on me. My teachers, friends, and parents had tried to tell me, especially my mother who did not think I should be in a relationship with this guy. My mom knew how much he meant to me and that I was taking our relationship seriously. Many times Mom told me, "Don't wait on him to call you or come to see you. You are too young for that. Have fun and enjoy your life. You have plenty of time to be committed to one man."

You cannot reason with a teen in love—especially me. You see, I had so much love for this young man; in my mind it was as if I already was married to him. We became the best of friends, and I think it was mostly because I never had sex with him. Though we dated for three years, I was unaware his "needs" were being met by other willing girls in town. Many times I caught him in lies about hanging out with other girls and found love letters, pictures—you name it. Each time I found out, it was like a bombshell, and the hurt would intensify. Each time he tried to make me believe his lying and cheating heart by telling or insinuating to me that it was basically my fault since I wouldn't have sex with him. Eventually I decided to give in to his sexual advances in the hope he would be true to me and only me.

It didn't work. Instead, I found myself not trusting him at all, especially when it came to the opposite sex. I think the only reason we lasted as long as we did was because we waited to have sex, and he truly got to know me, and it wasn't just for my body. My refusing to have sex evidently challenged him. In the process, he began to have a true love for me.

Though I felt he loved me, it still didn't help the nights of disappointment, his not calling and coming to see me, or the fact he kept me emotionally tied up as his girlfriend while he had his other girlfriends on the side.

It seemed I was crying most of the time and had never been so emotionally hurt in my entire life. Over and over again this guy deceived me, yet I really can't explain why I continued to listen to him. My only answer is that I truly believed I loved him so very much, and whenever I was with him, we had so much fun...not to mention that he was popular (a star athlete) in school. He knew just what to say to win my heart back over and over again. Looking back, I see I was such a naïve young girl.

Before the divorce, I had convinced myself I was the only girl in the world for him. In fact, he had a way of making me believe in him. I guess my reality was desensitized by his behavior, and I chose to ignore the emotional abuse for what it was.

* * *

In thinking back to before I went to kindergarten, I recall my first encounter with distrust for boys or men. I don't remember my exact age, but I do remember my mom taking me to the babysitter. Every day I would have to take a nap at the babysitter's. One time I woke up to find this older man touching me between my legs. I was so afraid and didn't want him to know I was awake. I barely breathed, not knowing what he was going to do to me. So, I pretended to be asleep, fearing his response if he suspected that I was awake. After that I never wanted to stay over there because of my experience with the babysitter's brother who appeared to be a child molester, the type of person you were taught to stay away from.

Day after day I would try to send signals to my mom that I didn't want to go over to the babysitter's house anymore. Being young and confused, I didn't know how to tell her what was happening to me at the babysitter's. My fear was that she would accuse me of making up the horrible stories about the babysitter's family member, and I worried that everyone would then hate me.

Just about every day I was subjected to this type of treatment. With time it increased to the point where he was making holes in the clothing so he could touch my private area. Whenever this happened, I closed my eyes and silently pleaded: *Please don't do anything else to me or hurt me.*

Since I didn't know what to do about the situation, I learned to put up with this treatment, which lasted until I no longer went to the babysitter's house anymore.

After that experience I was very wary and ever watchful, especially of the men and boys around me. Also, from then on, I was never able to take naps during the day. Intently observing the men around me, I noticed how they treated their wives or significant others. Strangely, I could tell when some men were being unfaithful. Others would tell lies while some just plain enjoyed getting drunk or using drugs.

For some strange reason, when the men were drinking, I got attention for being a "pretty little girl." Instead of making me feel pretty, I thought to myself: *What is wrong with these men? What am I doing that makes them notice me? Why do grown men want to feel-on an innocent little girl?*

* * *

Looking back, I see my zero trust level toward men started at an early age. That may be the reason upon first meeting my future husband; I felt he was the first real and true person I had met. He was loud and confident and everyone loved him. This made me think to myself: *Surely he is the best man I have ever met in my life!* Unfortunately, being young, impressionable, and with no experience, he soon shattered my hopes that he was a sincere, dependable, and trustworthy young man who would really care for and love me. This was especially hard on me after I had finally and willingly given my heart, for the first time.

Being in love, I tried to be blind to his faults because I wanted him to be all those things I yearned for in a young man. He not only took my heart, but also mistreated my trust and damaged it repeatedly with his deceitful and flirtatious ways. After him, I was left with absolutely no hope or trust in men and felt, if given a chance, any man would betray me or any woman for that matter.

Needless to say, that is how I came to believe all men were untrustworthy. Not knowing differently, I accepted that fact. To my immature way of thinking, I figured if a man were working, providing for his family, and he's not physically abusive or on drugs, then he must be a "good" man. From my observations it seemed it either didn't matter or the women didn't care enough to leave if a man was unfaithful. It was as if most of the women I observed were accepting of this way of married life.

I soon learned to overlook this "common" behavior from my future husband and forgave him each and every time. All he had to do was say he was sorry and make me feel like he really wanted me back. I found myself giving him the silent treatment for days or weeks depending on the situation because in my mind I needed to find a way to somehow punish him for his behavior. It was as if he were a child needing to be taught a lesson to do better or suffer the consequences. Sooner or later he would win back my heart. Over and over this happened in our relationship, thus becoming a classic pattern for us.

* * *

Ephesians 5:6-7 tells us:

> **Let no one deceive you with empty words, for because of such things God's wrath comes on those who are disobedient. Therefore do not be partners with them.**
>
> **(Ephesians 5:6-7 NIV)**

Soon we graduated from high school and went to college for a few years. At the time I was on my own, living as a young adult, going to college, and working. My future husband and I would visit each other often. While he was going to college in Weatherford on a football scholarship, I went to a junior college in Oklahoma City on a grant from the government because I was part Indian.

One winter night my future husband came to visit me. At the time I lived with two of my uncles on my mother's side of the family. They were not home at the time. I believe this was the night I conceived my first born, my son.

After giving birth to my son, my future husband and I soon moved in together. We both started jobs and established our family. During this time I was very happy even though we lived in a little shack. It didn't matter because we were in love. Being so happy, I felt as if I could live in a cardboard box with him if necessary. I was very content. However, it seemed every time I asked him to go with me somewhere that was of interest to me or to a family activity, he seldom wanted to attend. Thinking back, most of the time I attended events by myself.

One night I asked my future husband to go with me to a gathering my parents were having, and he said, "No, you go and I'll stay home and watch the baby." This would be the night more of his deceitful ways would come to light.

The next day I found out from one of the local girls that my future husband had betrayed me by taking our baby and another "girlfriend" to visit one of his college friends who lived out of town. I was furious that he would take another girl and our baby to visit his friends! *Oh, man,* I thought, *what a slap in the face. He must not care about me at all. I'm not even good enough to go with him to visit his friends as the mother of his child.*

That was the final straw. I finally had had enough and packed my stuff and left him. We had no contact for several months. During that time my son and I moved into an apartment with one of my girl cousins who was pregnant at the time. I decided I would not let my future husband treat me that way again, nor would I be his girlfriend ever again. If he wanted a relationship with our baby and me, it had to be a marriage. Nothing else would be acceptable.

In looking back and thinking about it, the only reason he actually married me was because I was adamant and refused to have it any other way.

The decision was made, and we decided to get married. The only thing I asked my soon-to-be husband was: "Make sure I am the woman you really want to marry and that you do not cheat or lie to me anymore. If you can't promise me that, then I don't want to marry you." I remember telling him I would be willing to wait until he was ready and that he could get all his playing around out of the way. It was important he understand I didn't want to be a part of that type of relationship anymore.

Glibly he assured me he was ready and he could be the husband and father to me and his son that I wanted. I was so excited and was able to put together a wedding in a matter of weeks.

* * *

On the day of our wedding, a feeling as if something was not right crossed my mind—I should not marry this man. I think in the back of my mind I feared he would not be faithful to me.

Another factor that had tested my resolve was when my fiancé was so negative about the minister of my youth, the pastor of the church I had attended growing up. He was the sweetest, kindest, and most soft-spoken person I had ever known. However, my fiancé didn't want him to do the marriage ceremony because he felt the man was too old and no one would be able to hear or understand him.

Though this was somewhat true, my feeling was that I wanted God to bless our marriage, and it shouldn't have been about his disappointment with my choice. After all, it was my big day, right? When he told me he didn't want the minister of my choice, it made me feel so bad my first thought was: *Maybe I should just back out now.* But then I thought: *How disappointed everyone will be if I call off the wedding; they wouldn't understand. Besides, if anyone deserves to be married to this man, I do if for no other reason than for all the crap he has put me through...and, I truly loved him.*

Ignoring the warning signs, I did get married, and we went back to our shack. The day was almost anticlimactic. I was so worn out I don't even think we made love that night, nor did we have a honeymoon.

My dream to be married to my high school sweetheart was fulfilled. I married the only man I had ever truly been in love with. My faith in our marriage working was all built on God's Word that once married, we would become one flesh.

Before getting married I knew my fiancé really only wanted to go to the courthouse for a quick, non-religious, impersonal

> **For this reason a man will leave his father and mother and he be united to his wife, and the two will become one flesh. So they are no longer two, but one. Therefore what God has joined together, let man not separate.**
>
> **(Matthew 19:5-6 NIV)**

ceremony. But I wanted what most young girls dream of—a church wedding where we recite our vows—you know, the I-do-for-better-or-worse-till-death-do-us-part ceremony.

Divorce Hurts: He Doesn't Want Me as His Wife Anymore

In my heart, I really felt I was the only woman made for him. But in looking back, I'm not sure if God was involved in our marriage at all. We never once went to church together; we didn't pray together; we didn't even have marriage counseling before the wedding.

Now, when looking back, I have had to ask myself: Was it true love for me? Was it just infatuation? Was it just the idea of doing the right thing? Was it the idea of being in love and having a family that made it feel so right at the time?

After our marriage all the family dynamics changed. I had plenty of in-laws and vice versa, and I would do anything for any of them. In truth, I don't think a family could have been any closer.

My mother in-law was the best in the world; a very sweet, loving woman whom I enjoyed talking to for hours. When I first met her, she already had multiple scleroses and spent a lot of her time in a wheel chair. The first thing that struck me about her was her sweet and loving spirit. She talked a lot about my husband's dad. I could tell she still loved him although they had been divorced and she had married another man. It is my personal belief that she loved him until the day of her death. Ironically his dad died the year following her death…I believe because he had truly loved her all those years too.

At that particular time in our marriage, I really felt like a part of his family, especially on his dad's side because most of our time together, before we married, had been spent at his uncle's house. Since that is where my husband had lived, it was natural we hung out over there most of the time.

I picked up on the fact that my husband's family had this "Hatfield and McCoy" relationship going on—his dad's family against his mom's family. At the time it just seemed they couldn't get along. But you could tell some of the girls in his mom's family liked the guys, and vice versa. Those relationships turned into marriages where they had children, and then ended in divorce too.

All in all, at the time, I felt like my husband was the best thing that could have happened to me. In my mind, I believed everything he told me because I was so in love for the very first time. Yet there truly was an illusion, because trusting was a major challenge for me when I had been disappointed time and time again. I could trust in him after marriage, knowing all the distrustful behaviors that scarred my heart. Yet, it felt so nice to be truly loved by someone whom I believed loved me and also needed my love.

Divorce Hurts: He Doesn't Want Me as His Wife Anymore

Step I—Love and Marriage

To help guide you through the healing process of divorce, explain your situation:

<u>What Happened?</u>

_____

_____

_____

_____

_____

_____

_____

_____

_____

_____

Your Feelings at the time:

What would you do differently?

_____

_____

_____

_____

_____

_____

_____

_____

_____

_____

_____

_____

CHAPTER 2
Marriage Built on Insecurities

Sometimes people find themselves so wrapped up with the idea of getting married that the real meaning and importance is lost. Women, think about it, how did your marriage proposal happen? Did he marry you out of obligation? Did he marry you because you were pregnant or you had children together? Did he marry you because you would be a good trophy wife, someone he could show off? Maybe you gave him a deadline or else that would be the end of the relationship? Or, did he ask you to be his wife...to love "only" you for a lifetime?

It's important to take marriage seriously and not accept being a charity case or put demands on your mate. Such situations only make things worse. These pressures may cause your mate to react from impulse or pressure because marriage will soon be threatened.

Then there are those in marriages who have their own hidden agendas. For instance, some people get married because they don't want anyone else raising their children, so they endure the relationship until their children get out of high school, and then it's their time to find true love and happiness. That's not a good situation to be in because the children never see true affection from mom and dad in the home and don't know what love really is. In this scenario the married couple usually puts on a good front outside the home as being a happy couple while inside their home, they are miserable. It's almost as if they were serving a prison sentence and were waiting for their sentence to be over so they can be free to find someone to love, or if it is a life sentence, to find friendships outside the home that would help them get through the years of loneliness and dissatisfaction that they have in their "marriage."

Think about it for a moment. Was it his choice to get married, or was it what you wanted to do? The man should be the one to find a wife and not be told who to marry or when. If a man truly loves a woman, he is willing to live his life with her and will know when the time is right.

Sometimes women are so desperate to find a mate to marry that they ignore the warning signs. Most girls dream and wonder about a fairytale wedding and the thought of being married. Women, don't sell yourself short; know what you are looking for in a mate. Be realistic with your expectations for a godly, faithful, and trustworthy man who can be the leader of his home.

* * *

> *He who finds a wife finds a good thing, and obtains favor from the Lord.*
>
> **(Proverbs 18:22 NKJV)**

Early in our marriage my husband had a tendency to fight, be disrespectful, and degrade me as he had learned at an early age how to treat a woman. I should have picked up on

Divorce Hurts: He Doesn't Want Me as His Wife Anymore

this behavior the first time he slapped me when we were in high school. The occasion was when I wanted him to get his class ring back from a girl to whom he had given it. It upset me she was wearing it, even though I was his girlfriend. He got mad at me because I demanded we go pick it up and he didn't want to do that. The only reason he did it was because I threatened to break up with him if he didn't.

There was another incident that happened at his uncle's house not long after we had been married. It started because all I wanted was for my son and me to go to my mom's house because my husband was drinking and playing dominos, which was a favorite pastime all through his growing-up years. I was crying because we were fighting. In anger and frustration, my husband picked me up, threw me from his uncle's porch, and tried to lock me out of the house. But he didn't have the last word. Before he finished, I managed to fight back and ended up giving him a black eye...what a horrible experience with someone you cherish and love.

His uncle was a man who always had women and was a great entertainer. At that time I don't think he had ever committed to one woman, not that I saw. I was beginning to believe my husband was the next generation that had been cursed with this particular behavior. Some men learn by example to keep their wife in line with physical or emotional abuse. Others, by example, learn it is good to have as much sex with as many women as possible.

After my husband mistreated me, I told him we might as

well get a divorce because I refused to let a man physically abuse and mistreat me. I added that I had found out his father and uncle had physically abused their wives and had been unfaithful to them until the wives had had enough, and the marriages ended in divorce.

As I think back, our situation reminded me of how my dad and mom would argue, and my mom seemed to be the best private investigator in the world. Mom worked twenty-four hours a day it seemed to support her family, even when my dad didn't have or couldn't find a job. During these times it was hard not only on my dad but on all of us. He drowned his sorrows in liquor and had buddies who helped him accomplish this goal on many occasions.

Many times I observed my mom looking for and finding my dad around the city. Many times he was in places and with women he shouldn't have been with as well. At those times I remember thinking to myself: *Why does she stay with him? Why does she strive so hard to keep our family together? What is the point?*

Looking back I don't recall ever seeing my mom and dad acting in a loving way or even kissing each other. In my heart and mind, I figured that to have children you had to be engaged in some type of romantic relationship. As I think about it, I never received any real affection from my dad. I don't remember any hugs or kisses; he just didn't show he cared...when he was sober. But when he got drunk, it was another story. At those times I could hardly stand his behavior or the attention—that's when I heard the famous words, "I love you".

He could also be crude. After I started dating and would return home from a date, he would ask me, "Are you still a virgin?"

That's one thing I was always proud to answer, "Yes!" Yet I wondered if my dad really remembered our conversation in the morning.

When I had a chance to observe and compare, I realized the behavior in both our families was very similar, and surprisingly, everyone seemed to accept it as "normal." It seemed all they did was smoke, drink, and have a good time all weekend long and sometimes even through the week. It just depended on the reason or excuse.

After that time when he threw me off the porch, and I had my say, my husband vowed never to lay another hand on me because he didn't want to be like his dad or uncle. He said he didn't want to treat me in the same way they treated women.

In looking back I think that was the last time we had a physical fight. However, the sarcastic insults and cursing never ended during our entire relationship.

Trying to better understand my husband and myself, I have since learned people who hide behind insults and abusive language are more than likely insecure, fearful, or have guilt that tempts them to protect themselves at the expense of another person. Abusive language reveals a sinful heart.

Divorce Hurts: He Doesn't Want Me as His Wife Anymore

For whatever reason, I feel something must have clicked inside him after I unloaded on him. After that he seemed ready to be a husband to me and a father to our son.

Something else that seemed to help our situation came shortly after when he began working at a welding company, and I got a job working nights for UPS. This really helped us out because it was a perfect job scenario, and we didn't have to pay childcare.

Things were going so well, I started feeling as if our marriage was really going to work. We became a family, and even upgraded our living conditions and our vehicle. Our first real home was a trailer in a trailer park. One of his aunts graciously co-signed, along with his dad, for us to get a car. It was thrilling. I had my first brand new car, which my husband picked out just for me. Deep down inside I knew my husband was trying to do the best he could to love me in the only way he knew how.

I remember things going great, and then suddenly my husband lost his job. The aimless pattern began to repeat itself—drinking, smoking, and playing dominos to fill the time, while I was the only one working.

At the time I didn't understand how close we were living to one of our classmates, his best friend's brother. I'll refer to him throughout the story as his best friend's brother, who at the time stayed right across the street from us in the trailer park.

Day in day out I'd get up and go to work, and while my

husband would seem to enjoy his days being off work, it began to wear on me. I realized the situation was not working for me. My husband would have to get a job and work too. I really didn't care if it was at a fast food restaurant, even though he still received unemployment money.

After several months of being unemployed, my husband decided to try and make a living in Texas since I already had an aunt and uncle living in Dallas, which was fine with me as I had always been able to count on them.

He left first to find employment and then he sent for the baby and me. I hadn't realized until I got to Texas and we were on our own, that my husband's best friend's brother was also in Dallas. His friend helped us find our first apartment. Though it was the only thing we could afford, it was in a less-than-desirable part of the city. But, still in love with my husband, I would have followed him anywhere. It really didn't matter as long as I was with him.

My husband had a free spirit and very easily made friends at his jobs, around the apartment—anywhere. He was just a very likable guy.

When we moved from Oklahoma to Texas, leaving the only family with which I had been familiar, it wasn't long before one of my brothers-in-law followed. He stayed with us. We had a one-bedroom apartment, were barely making ends meet, and yet decided to help my younger brother-in-law.

Actually, I didn't mind. That was one thing my husband and I had in common—helping family.

Soon my sister-in-law called and said she needed our help as well. We had four adults and a three-year-old all staying in a one-bedroom apartment. This was difficult on our marriage, but we were determined to provide the support. Things were tight because we didn't ask for any money from them. Both my husband and I wanted to help them get on their feet so they could get their own place and become independent. We were the oldest siblings and wanted to help in any way possible.

Then when I thought things could not get any worse, I ran out of birth-control pills. I didn't have a doctor in Texas yet and figured it would be okay as my husband and I hadn't been sexually active except once for a whole month. Since I had been on birth-control pills for three years, I didn't even think about getting pregnant.

Eventually I found out about a clinic and scheduled a visit with Planned Parenthood since I didn't have any health insurance. I was looking forward to my visit so I could get more birth control pills. After the necessary exam and test, the doctor came back in the room and said with a smile, "You're pregnant!"

Totally shocked, I began to cry, thinking: It must be a joke. We had sex only one time! No, no, it can't be true...

When I left the office, uppermost in my mind was the thought: *I simply will have to get an abortion. We can't even afford a better place right now, and we're barely making it.*

With a sad heart I went home and waited for my husband

to come home. I remember telling him the news. "I'm pregnant." Needless to say, he was not happy and felt the same way—we didn't need another baby. Then his next words shocked me when he asked, "By whom?"

I told him, "You are so insensitive to my feelings. I can't believe you have the nerve to ask me that. I have never given you any reason to doubt my faithfulness to you. So why would you ask me that?"

He replied, "Because we only had sex one time the whole month." For him to ask, "By who?" would insinuate it's not his.

If there was one thing of which I was sure, it was that he was the one who got me pregnant. It was his heartless sarcasm that was more harmful than physical bruises. My husband was the master at being sarcastic to me most of the time. His attitude and comments really hurt me, and I cried a lot because it appeared my husband would not take any ownership for his part in the pregnancy.

> ***Reckless words pierce like a sword, but the tongue of the wise brings healing.***
>
> **(Proverbs 12:18 NIV)**

It seemed to me that the blame was mine alone. His attitude towards me, which I felt, was "How could you let this happen?" and "Why did it happen?"

I didn't know what to do and felt so alone in my decision. Then I wrote a letter to my grandmother on my mom's side of the family. I explained our situation and told her I didn't see any way we could keep this child and that I was actually thinking about having an abortion (even though I really didn't believe in abortions). It was just that the situation seemed so dark and I couldn't see any way out, and my husband was not helping the situation one bit with his accusing attitude.

My grandmother wrote me back and in short, told me to have the child because she had had seventeen children, and God was not going to give me more than I could bear. She advised me to pray about it, assuring me that everything was going to work out just fine.

After her letter, I accepted my pregnancy and began to pray for my child's health and wellbeing. I also prayed for a little girl and told God that if I was blessed with one, I'd make sure I didn't get pregnant ever again.

> *Has not the Lord made them one? In flesh and spirit they are his. And why one? Because he was seeking godly offspring. So guard yourself in your spirit, and do not break faith with the wife of your youth.*
>
> **(Malachi 2:15 NIV)**

God was so gracious to bless us with two wonderful children including the little girl my heart so desired. And I'm joyful to know that they both know and love the Lord!

Step II—Marriage Built on Insecurities
To help guide you through the healing process of divorce, explain your situation:

<u>What Happened?</u>

_____

_____

_____

_____

_____

_____

_____

_____

_____

Divorce Hurts: He Doesn't Want Me as His Wife Anymore

Your Feelings at the time:

What would you do differently?

CHAPTER 3
Issues of Marriage

In trying to figure where and when things really began to go wrong in our marriage, I keep coming back to that evening when I told my husband I was pregnant for the second time. His immediate, insensitive response of, "By who?" seemed to kill something in me. From then on, that kept going around and around in my mind, causing me not only to resent him for that question; it made it even harder for me to trust him as far as having my best interests in mind.

Maybe the reason for the question was that I never really wanted to have sex, because from working, keeping our household together, and being exhausted most of the time, it was a lot for a young working mother. But it was not because I didn't love my husband. My husband was a wonderful man, father, and provider for his family whom I cherished.

Eventually he accepted the fact of the pregnancy, and we went on with our lives. Yet all throughout my pregnancy I seemed to stay angry and resentful. In addition to my negative personal feelings about having no attention or privacy in our young marriage, my brother-in-law, sister-in-law, and husband seemed to be enjoying themselves constantly by playing dominos and talking crazy to one another during those times. Though it was mostly in love and fun, it went on day in and day out and began to stress me out and made my nerves bad during my pregnancy. Yes, I know they never knew it because it was a cause and effect of being pregnant and sometimes our hormones tend to go crazy.

Soon afterwards my in-laws moved out and were able to get an apartment together and established their own living arrangements. My brother- and sister-in-law didn't move too far away, and I was glad they were close to us because we truly had a deep love for each other and still do.

After their move, when my husband was at work or gone from the apartment, I found myself alone and not in a happy frame of mind. I would cook, clean, and wash the clothes. At the time we could not afford a washer and dryer, and I remember hauling clothes out to the car and then into the laundromat each week. Since there was no one to assist me with either the children or chores, and I didn't expect any help, I always just did the best I could.

My husband sometimes worked two jobs, so I usually didn't get much help from him earlier within our marriage. If he was at home and not working, he would pick up the slack with the children, washing the clothes, or doing chores that needed to be done, not to mention being a great cook. My husband was a very hard-working man, very dependable and reliable, and true to his job or jobs so he could provide for us.

Needing more room, my husband and I moved into a two-bedroom apartment that was upstairs in the same apartment complex. Though it gave us more room, I now had to haul both the dirty and clean clothes and groceries up and down the stairs during my pregnancy...and the endless doctor appointments. Soon after, our daughter was born.

Though we were on a tight income, I am proud to say we paid for rent, food, and clothing, and we survived! I handled all the bills, and my husband had no problem handing his paycheck(s) over to me. He knew I would handle everything correctly.

Never was I happier than the day we decided to move out of those apartments. In looking around, we found a nicer, two-bedroom apartment in Irving, Texas.

* * *

That same year, one of my husband's younger brothers decided to divorce his wife and shortly afterwards began a relationship with an old girlfriend from his old hometown. Their relationship progressed rapidly and before we knew it, he was married again.

Anything I had or any place where we lived, I didn't mind sharing anything with my husband's family, nor my own side of the family.

It was during that same year my husband began having problems becoming sexually aroused. In other words, he couldn't have sex. He told me he was having a problem getting blood pumping in his libido. But when I tried to arouse him for the first time, he actually turned me down when I reached out to him to have sex (yes it actually happened). I was so shocked I didn't know quite what to think because I'm sure it shocked him that I even tried. Then I figured he must have been sleeping around on me. After all, we were only in our twenties! Are you kidding me? Maybe it was because, I was never really interested in sex or initiated wanting sex, and it was just something I didn't think about.

To make things worse, about that time he lost his job and we were again struggling to make it. To add to the mix, two of his close male friends separated from their wives and decided to move to Texas. Soon, they started coming over regularly while I was at work. The dominos and drinking started all over again.

In the middle of all this, we now had a son and daughter to care for, and the roles soon reversed—my husband was now doing all the chores while I was at work. However, I always handled the bills and made sure everything was paid, as he didn't have a head to budget the money.

Busy with a new baby girl, a young son, a house to run, and basically most of the responsibilities on my shoulders, I began to realize my husband and I were drifting farther and farther apart. It seemed I was losing his interest. He was hanging out with his friends and also with his best friend's brother more than usual. Our communication was not on the same level. I felt he was out and about, making more and more friends while I was working and staying home, and alone with the children. I'm sure he was ready to get out of the house after I would come home from work.

All of a sudden, my husband's best friend's brother moved into a new house. About that time we moved to another apartment in the Dallas area to be closer to my husband's family and friends. This marked a major change in our marriage. As I look back, that year and the many changes and circumstances were the beginning of the end of our first marriage.

Fortunately, a short time after our move to Dallas, my husband found another job.

My oldest brother-in-law had gotten remarried, and it seemed my husband was excited about their relationship and enjoyed reminiscing frequently about their childhood days with his brother's wife than focusing on us. They all seemed to have a close relationship, and I felt left out of this part of my husband's life. To top it off, about 1988 his baby brother from his mother's second marriage was "dropped-off" for us to rear. This was when his mother was placed into a nursing home for several years. Although I loved my husband's whole family, I was not ready for this challenge in my life. Since my husband and I were the oldest siblings and most responsible of the family, it sort of just fell on us to help raise him.

Often I felt alone in my efforts to rear him. My husband was hardly ever there because of working, and it seemed to me I was always home cooking, cleaning, washing clothes, and taking care of my son, baby daughter, and now my very young brother-in-law. It left me feeling very overwhelmed with rearing two young children and an eleven-year-old. I felt frustrated that no one was trying to help and support me. I felt the older members of the family should have taken more responsibility to help me and help him. I wanted my husband to handle it...to let them know. And, since I was married to my husband it seemed it was my obligation to make it all work. I understood it was not an easy life for any of us, especially my husband's siblings, having a mother who suffered from an illness, helping take care of her from a very young age, and having a father that was not supportive to them. We were all we had and we survived! After a period of time my sister-n-law decided to step in and help take over parenting my brother-in-law. And, in the end, the Lord has a way of putting everyone in place to fulfill his plan for our lives.

> *If God is for us, who can be against us?*
>
> **(Roman 8:31 NKJV)**

My baby brother in law was returned to his father, who never wanted to be apart from his son, and he turned out to be very blessed and a fine young man.

During that experience, I began letting Satan have my thoughts of retaliation. Here I was, crying for help, yet no one listened to me; especially my husband. He either didn't understand my feelings or didn't care what I was trying to tell him. Plainly, my husband was not listening to me, or I just didn't know how to tell him. All he focused on was that I didn't trust him, or I was jealous, neither of which was the issue.

Soon, I found myself daydreaming and wondering: *What if I hurt my husband like he has hurt me? Would he be able to stand the pain I had endured from all his crap?* After those thoughts, I began looking at other men differently because for so long my husband had had my total attention. In all our marriage, I had never contemplated being with anyone else except my husband. My love for him was very real, even though at one point he suggested to one of his friends that he ought to have sex with me because then I would get it out of my system, and he wouldn't have to worry about it anymore.

Now, I never accepted his craziness, but it caused me to lose friendships because the perception of my character was judged, even though I had never had any intention of having sex with his friend or friends.

One of my first thoughts to myself when my husband suggested this was: *Why doesn't my husband care if I have sex with his friend? Why would he seriously contemplate the idea and talk to his friend and then his friend asked his wife?*

What an insult this suggestion was to me. It proved only to

add more strain on our already weak marriage.

Second, after thinking about it, I really don't think my ex-husband and I ever had any quality time together, like a chance to enjoy each other alone. Instead, it seemed someone was always around or staying with us. As a matter of fact, at one point or another in our marriage, all of our siblings from his side (6) and my side (4) lived with us, not to mention other family and friends. Looking back, we should have invested more time with each other first to build up a strong foundation in marriage, instead of adding more challenges and struggles to our relationship. I know, we just wanted to help support our family, and we did just that!

Third, I knew that financially we were drowning in debt; we had to pay for daycare for two children and keep our bills paid on top of that. The cost of living was more than we both expected, and we had low-paying jobs.

Fourth, was our communication or lack thereof. It suffered greatly because we hardly ever saw each other, or specifically we had no alone-time in which to share our lives with each other.

More and more I felt disconnected from my husband. He had made many new friends while I had made only one real friend. She was a sweet, Hispanic young woman there in Texas.

Definitely, this was not a good situation in which we found ourselves. Daily, I felt the disappointment, and slowly resentment in me grew over his relationships with all his family and friends. It seemed he had nothing left to give me, and I felt so alone.

Step III—Issues of Marriage
To help guide you through the healing process of divorce, explain your situation:

What Happened?

_____

_____

_____

_____

_____

_____

_____

_____

_____

Divorce Hurts: He Doesn't Want Me as His Wife Anymore

Your Feelings at the time:

Divorce Hurts: He Doesn't Want Me as His Wife Anymore

What would you do differently?

CHAPTER 4
Dealing with Guilt

For the first time, in regards to my marriage, I made a very poor decision which allowed Satan to be at his best in my life. Though I was asking for help in my mind, maybe I just didn't know how to ask for help. I felt neglected, and it seemed no one was there for me. Now I know the devil wanted me to believe that, and, yes, I fell for the lies. My rationale was: *This is your life; deal with it. Your husband doesn't care and your family doesn't care. All your husband wants and enjoys is hanging out with his friends and co-workers, lusting after single women, and watching nude videos.* In my mind I told myself: *Just do what you need to do to make yourself feel better.*

To me "better" was if I stopped caring about my husband's feelings because he was taking me for granted. It seemed his behavior was not desirable, and yet he trusted me with his heart. My husband believed I would never be unfaithful or have a relationship with anyone behind his back. To me, it felt as if in some ways he was somewhat cocky, trusting me that much, which is a great thing for a relationship, but I viewed it as taking me for granted. This had to be the turning point in our marriage.

Then the humiliation started not just for me, but also for my husband. I let him/us down and others when I didn't live up to my morals and beliefs. The devil had convinced me I should hurt him as he had hurt me. It was important for him to know what it felt like to be disrespected. My concern was that my husband would be the only man in the world to have my heart, and he hadn't done a very good job in taking care of it.

It all began one summer in August. I went to a rodeo in Okmulgee and actually was thinking: *God, let me find someone attractive to be with.* Why was I asking God for this, especially being married and bonded to my husband for life? In looking back, the reality is that Satan gave me exactly what I wanted.

As soon as I hit the small town, family members greeted me with the news that an old friend was looking for me. This man had always liked me, but I had never given him the time of day because for me, it was all about my husband. Having gone into the Army and now having just returned home, he was evidently looking for me. Wow, it was heavy news! Someone was actually looking for me!

Right from the first, my eyes were deceived. Everything about him seemed perfect—he had a nice body; good looks, and I had never really noticed him before as I did that night. I actually believed he was heaven-sent, just because it was all such perfect timing.

Now I see things more clearly. Satan was using this old friend to destroy my family, everything my husband believed about me, and what others believed about me. You see, I had always held my standards high when it came to cheating on your partner or spouse. I was a living advocate to save everyone that I saw was getting played.

But lo and behold, the same thing would end up happening to me. When the relationship started out, it was fun and interesting. I had someone there, just for me. He listened to my problems about my life. I enjoyed his company and lived as if I had no regard for my husband. At this point, I had not given into the sexual act, but my husband found out about this old friend from a relative. My husband asked me about the relationship and I was honest and told the truth. After, that he began to accuse me of having sex with the man and would not let it go.

For a long time I struggled with the resentment of everything my husband had done to me, and I justified my actions with this idea: *If he is going to accuse me of something I might as well make it a reality.* If my husband suggested giving his wife to his best friend, something was seriously wrong. Evidently he didn't care about me.

Obviously my husband's thinking was very different from mine. There are certain things I would not do, and one is that I would NEVER suggest or ask another woman to be with my husband. So, in my mind, I had justification for my actions, and the very moment I gave in to adultery was the very moment I let the devil defeat me. It was all because I felt my husband was taking me for granted, and I didn't feel or receive any love from him. For so long I had been doing everything possible to support our family, and no credit was being given. The attitude was always like, "So what?" My slip seemed to surprisingly satisfy others in my family that, yes, she finally did something wrong. I was living and breathing in the world of adultery, a very sinful act that is not of God.

I know it was nothing but the devil himself that had stirred up my discontent. The saying in the Bible is so true—what's done in the dark will eventually come to the light.

I wondered, just maybe, if I wanted him to find out. Maybe my whole purpose had been to get him to notice me and show me some love.

The cause and effect didn't happen as I had planned. The consequences destroyed a perfectly good relationship as I knew it to be. We just needed to communicate and listen to each other in order to meet each other halfway and look up to God. Although I grew up going to church, I was not going to church with my family.

Naturally, after my betrayal, things were never the same between us. I felt like Adam and Eve in the Garden of Eden. The serpent wanted me to believe this affair was what I needed to do. All my holiness in our marriage was destroyed, and it was because of me. I had gotten caught eating from the forbidden tree when clearly God's scripture tells us:

> ***Thou shall not commit adultery.***
>
> **(Exodus 20:14 KJV)**

Before my affair, it seemed to me everyone acted as if nothing was wrong in their marriages. Some spouses knew their spouse was cheating, and others didn't, and it didn't seem to matter. If someone told them the truth, thinking they were helping the situation, they were looked upon as a troublemaker and out to destroy their good thing, yet his or her marriage survived.

All of a sudden, my eyes were opened, and I lost my innocence. The sinful act had destroyed everything in which I had believed. The guilt was more than I could handle. My moral character and values in my beliefs had been tested and I had failed horribly, contaminating my vows.

The guilt and shame slowly began killing all my beliefs of who I was and what I believed in. For a time it seemed as though I gave up on myself. I wanted to be like the perception of everyone else, just living as if I had no fear or respect for my life or myself. Now my good name had been flawed, and I was no longer the person I had been proud to be or wanted to be. The things I did were no one's fault but my own—this I had to accept. I had to look in the mirror and realize I could never criticize my husband again for his actions when I had turned around and done the very same thing to him that had hurt me the most throughout our relationship. It was as if I had picked up his bad habits and could not control the person I had become. Yet, at the same time, I figured he deserved everything I had dished out. No longer did I care or have regard or respect for his feelings.

The careless choice I made to hurt the man I loved would change my whole life. Also, it would affect the goal I had worked so hard to reach, which was to treat everyone as I would want him or her to treat me. This one simple statement was a part of the person I had always tried to be, but I had not stayed true to myself.

Suddenly, it struck me right between the eyes: once you make a choice to hurt someone because he or she has hurt you, you can't take it back. After I clearly saw myself and better understood the ramifications of what I had done, I knew it was going to take God to get me back on the right track.

This I learned: **Sin Always Affect Others!** The sin takes you through three steps:

1. Contemplation—wanting to do it, focusing on it, how to do it.

2. Rationalization—thinking it's okay, they deserve it, and they did it to you.

3. Consent—giving into the sinful act, deceived/defeated by the devil.

In our society today, Christians are being led down the wrong path by deception of the devil because it looks and feels good. But trust in God to tell you the truth, because everything the devil offers you is a lie to deceive you and take you to unfamiliar territory that you know nothing about. The devil wants to destroy you so don't listen to your emotions, to your desires, to this world, and especially the devil. Listen to God's Word and to the Holy Spirit.

Even after all my sinful acts, I still believed God cared about me. He cared about my defeat, and He cared about my feelings. So I found a church to start attending that was near our first starter home, and this was the beginning of my healing process. I was also baptized during my fellowship and walk in faith.

> *Out of the depths I cry to you, O Lord; O Lord, hear my voice. Let your ears be attentive to my cry for mercy. If you, O Lord, kept a record of sins, O Lord, who could stand? But with you there is forgiveness; therefore you are feared.*
>
> **(Psalm 130:1-4 NIV)**

Step IV—Dealing with Guilt

To help guide you through the healing process of divorce, explain your situation:

How do you deal with the guilt?
- Admit It
- Own It
- Deal With It
- Acknowledge It
- Repent

_____

_____

_____

_____

_____

_____

_____

Divorce Hurts: He Doesn't Want Me as His Wife Anymore

Your Feelings at the time:

_____

_____

_____

_____

_____

_____

_____

_____

_____

_____

What would you do differently?

Testimony

I first met my husband in a church at a crusade. He was on the stage bringing people of all ages to Christ.

> *So then faith comes by hearing, and hearing by the Word of God.*
>
> **(Romans 10:17 NKJV)**

It was turmoil from the beginning. Looking back, I should have never answered the phone the next time he called or replied to the next text. But then, would I have been able to have experienced the full grace of God as I have over the past three years?

When I first met my husband, I wasn't looking to date. What caught me was that he appeared and acted to be a Christian man, at first. Two months into long phone conversations and emails, his girlfriend called me at work. Girlfriend... almost fiancée, being that he had been looking at rings the prior week!!! That should have been my first clue, but when he told me that God had ordained us to be together and he was about to break it off with her, I believed and trusted him. After all who was SHE to be telling me the 'lies' that he told her that I was stalking him? She was the 'liar' because she wasn't even a Christian before she met him. He brought her to Jesus. Also, I was "lucky" to have a "good Christian man" like him. What good Christian man would want an old washed-up stripper who was a single mom with a child? He would often tell me my looks were fading, and I was too scrawny, so I needed him, or so I allowed him to make me feel and think like this. Once I started to realize it was not true, out came the manipulation and spiritual abuse. He could have me so convinced that I was not saved and that I was nothing without him, a man of God, that I felt embarrassed to read my Bible anymore.

When someone tells you that you are spiritually immature, time in and time out when you speak of God, and you aren't allowed to meet his friends or coworkers, one begins to doubt oneself. My ex-husband would play nice, and we would have deep conversations in the beginning. I told him everything about my life. He, in turn, would use my past against me, to rip and tear me and my self esteem down. One Wednesday night in church, God tried to warn me. I was in praise and deeply in worship. My ex had hacked into my email and found pictures of me of a time that I was at a friend's house before I had even met my ex-husband. He was calling me names no man should call a woman, much less one human being to another as I sat in the church parking lot. He would call me names because I went out with athletes of a different race than his. He would not talk to me for days and tell me I made him sick and I was a liar all because I spilled out my past to him.

In praise and worship, I found the strength to raise my hands and I cried. I felt not worthy; after all my ex-husband had been telling me I was a "this and that," reminding me of my past. This from a "man of God" who stands on stages week after week "bringing people to Christ." I wasn't worthy. God showed me otherwise that Wednesday night. I got a swift mental image of a hand coming out and taking, leading me away from something. That week my friends did an intervention. They took my phone for a week. But the words he instilled in my mind were cemented. I felt like I was nothing and was so afraid that he was going to find someone better or younger than I. Again, I felt I should be lucky to have him. He is a Christian man. I wouldn't find another, so he had me convinced.

I ended up moving to Dallas in August of 2006. While I drove to Dallas, he would not answer his phone. The last time I spoke to him, he'd mentioned that his ministry friends wanted him to meet and date Dallas Cowboy cheerleaders who were recently saved by the grace of God, and told me I had better "hurry and get there"!

He had me so convinced that it was the works of man on earth that made God's face shine upon you and bless you! Then I came across a book, *Spiritual Battles,* that gave me the seeds of desire and power to read my Bible again! Drenched with Bible verses, I started to realize I had allowed my ex-husband to use the Bible incorrectly. I had allowed a sliver of a crack for the enemy to slither in and take over!

Well, now that I realized it, I was prepared to kick the enemy out on his rear again and strengthen my walls of protection. For this battle, I needed my amour! I needed the word, in truth from GOD, not from man. I began fasting and praying, and praying, and more praying. I learned how to pray and pray hard! I started to talk to God everyday—all day! Sometimes the prayers were short and sporadic, but I was continually in prayer. Soon my ex-husband proposed. He put on an act that he had changed. While time got closer for us to go to Jamaica to wed, true colors revealed again. With my new confidence in God and His Word, I would question my ex-husband which only led to my not being submissive OR he was stressed out. Once we were married, he would "be fine" (which is what he would say).

We followed through with the marriage, and I got pregnant on our honeymoon. I told him the good news, and he denied the baby was his, and then kicked me and my daughter out. I was shocked and devastated about how he treated us.

We tried to work it out with the help of friendly counsel, but after learning more lies about him and his past and infidelity, I filed for divorce in January 2007. Four months after we were married, the mental and spiritual abuse was too much to endure. Almost two years to the day that we were married, a few months shy of being a two-year ongoing a divorce case, the divorce was final. After Family Court Evaluations and court dates pushed it out for two years, it was "proofed up" and final.

I chose to quit complaining and entertaining the situation by speaking about it. I crawled into Jesus' arms with my Bible and notebook in hand. The enemy was NOT happy with that. I thought to myself that I know I am not to question God, "Why me, God, why?", but to ask, "What God, what? Which way God, which way?" However, God's plan has not and will not be derailed! God revealed to me that I am not to allow anyone to deceive me with empty words (Ephesians 5:6). God instructs us to guard our hearts, (Proverbs 4:23). This is the wellspring of life, where God communicates to you through Christ.

I quit reading all emails from my ex. I did not continue a conversation with him if he turned it into an argument. I had to retrain my brain. God instructs us to control our minds. I learned to replace my thoughts. Philippians 4:7 instructs us to guard our hearts and our minds in Christ Jesus. I retrained my mind to redirect on thoughts of what was good, lovely, and admirable and to appreciate what was good around me. Philippians 4:8 instructs about what we are to keep our minds set on. It tells us to put our mind in practice and the God of Peace will be with you. Once you get a taste of peace it is like no other! The forgiveness flows, the love flows, and the faith flows. I am ready to move onward and upward to help others who have endured hardships.

Some paths are painful, but so was the crucifixion for our Savior. It is the least we can do to learn, what would Jesus do? How would Jesus....? If Jesus can forgive those who whipped him and tortured him, I can overcome and forgive...because He lives in ME! God can heal the hurt and will fill your emptiness, it is up to you to feed and water the "want" of that feeling of emptiness by handing it over to God and turning your full face to Him. Not by having God in one hand and your situation in the other and going back and forth from hand to hand; give your situation to God! Reach toward the future with both hands! If you are holding your situation in one hand, that doesn't give God the assurance in Him that you give your trust!

Carrie Johnson

> *Those who know your name will trust in you, for you, Lord have never forsaken those who seek you.*
>
> **(Psalm 9:10 NIV)**

CHAPTER 5
Feelings of No Respect

After I was baptized and had accepted the Lord as my Savior, things appeared as if I was on the right track—then the devil got busy again. It seemed when I was trying to do good, evil was all around me.

Some Sunday mornings I would get up and ask my husband to go to church with our children and me. It was always the same answer, "No."

Our house had become the weekend hangout for my husband, his friends, and our relatives with dominos, drinking, and cursing--the main entertainment, which usually ended with fights. It seemed that weekend after weekend this was what we did for entertainment.

Instead of enjoying the "entertainment," I was frustrated and didn't know how to get my husband to start going to church and fellowship with other Christians in the house of the Lord. To my way of thinking, if we did this, it might help change our lives for the better.

My husband told me he didn't trust the men at churches and refused to have anything to do with the church or anyone connected with it.

The attacks on my family increased, and I began to hear rumors my husband was having an affair with a young lady from our hometown. This change came about the same time my husband began staying out late at night after work or going on all-night fishing trips. Yet I never saw any fish or smelled the odor of fish when he finally made it home. Then the final straw seemed to be when he began having manhood problems and not being able to have sex with me again. I thought: *Here we go again.* Although I didn't have any proof, I knew something was going on; I just could not prove it.

I decided to join a church in a suburb of Dallas and rededicated my life to the Lord. I really wanted my husband to join and be a part of leading his family, but he wanted no part of church. It seemed I was on the right track living for the Lord and then the devil got busy attacking our relationship again. Soon, I found myself finding friendships at work and hanging out with my co-workers, who happened to be mostly men. However, I would invite my friends (strictly friends) over to meet my husband. He had always said he wanted me to get a life and have friends like him—male or female, it didn't matter. My husband had all types of friends, and I met them as if he had nothing to hide and was innocent. But now it was my turn to have friends. I don't think he cared for me having single male friends. It affected our relationship.

In spite of all my new friends, I began to feel a sense of betrayal again, although I couldn't see it. To add to that, my husband came up with the same excuse again of his manhood, not being able to make love to me. I began to believe things were not going to work and shared with him that I wanted a divorce and the reasons why.

Divorce Hurts: He Doesn't Want Me as His Wife Anymore

Always, I had had a problem trying to talk to my husband. It seemed my words would get twisted. If I really wanted to state my feelings, I would write a letter to my husband. The following is part of a letter I gave to him to help my husband understand my feelings:

> *I'm sorry we have made a mess out of our marriage. But, I'm finally ending this ugly relationship. I love you and I always will. But, after my mistake in our marriage you have just not been the man I married. I believe you love me but you have no respect for me and I can't go through life with a man who has no respect for his own wife. You have been a great supporter and father. It's time to move on to happier times with someone you can respect. I'm doing this for our kids and me. How can they have respect for me when you don't? I've tried, you've tried, but, let's face it, we're not happy with each other. So, you won't leave, fine, I will. I hope you are happy.*
>
> *Love, No respect.*

Instead of giving it to him, I left the letter in a convenient location for him to find. I'm not sure if he read the letter or not before I placed it in my Bible. These were the things I had wanted to say, but was sure I would never give the letter to him (directly). I just needed to get my feelings out and writing it down helped me.

The next thing that happened, which drastically changed our life, occurred in the month of May of 1992. My husband decided to leave me and left me this note saying:

I had loaded my stuff on the truck but couldn't leave. I asked the Lord for guidance. I opened the Bible to this letter. I guess this is the sign. Maybe later, after I've located my manhood, we can try again. I know you're the woman for me. Maybe just not right now. (It had a drawing of an unhappy face.)

You see I had never intended on giving my husband the letter, and if I did, now I would never get the chance to leave him or tell him because he had found the letter and decided to leave me. The only reason I had written it was to get my feelings out and the only way I knew how was to write it down and put it in my Bible. You see, I wanted to pray about it before I made any hasty decision because I realized that I had a chemical imbalance each and every month right before my cycle would start. During those times I could not control my thoughts or feelings. When I had written that letter I had been having a bad bout of PMS (premenstrual syndrome). After each episode I would feel sorry for my husband. I just couldn't control my feelings. It seemed all the things that bothered me about him and our relationship would surface month after month, and at the time it seemed larger than life.

However, it seemed my husband was more than ready to accommodate my wishes, from a letter that I had put in my Bible. I actually think it was the devil having his way. I don't think the Lord would have my husband leave me and his children to go stay with his best friend's brother after he divorced his second wife; then he would proceed to help my husband find a way to divorce me. Wow, my husband moved in with his best friend's brother and let this man help him to divorce me. I guess during this time I was okay because I knew something wasn't right, and all the hometown gossip about him messing around was true because he ended up with this woman after our divorce.

The divorce was soon filed the first time around. I then learned that there was a question about my husband possibly being the father of one of this woman's children. At that time, I gave up all hope on our marriage and did not see a future for us. But my husband soon advised me he didn't want a divorce, but I was not trying to hear him or trust him anymore. I just wanted him to get the divorce.

The divorce was final in November of 1992. We lost our home because alone I could no longer afford to pay the mortgage. After we lost our home, I first moved into an apartment in Mesquite with my daughter. My ex-husband and son moved in with the best friend's brother. Now, as I think back on it, I'm not really sure how the split affected our children. Not only were their parents separated but they also would be separated from each other, just to accommodate us.

I really didn't know how I was going to move forward, but I was not going to let him get the best of me. With head held high, I was confident in my ability to find someone else to love me. After all, I was still young and had a strong desire to succeed in life. The main thing that gave me comfort was that I knew God was going to take care of my children and me. In faith, I believed everything would be all right.

Soon I started dating, and things were going well until my ex-husband brought another woman over to my apartment to pick up my son who was visiting with me for the weekend. I was totally blown away! He had absolutely no consideration for my feelings, and it left me feeling very upset and hurt. Furious, I went to my car to get a hammer to break all the windows out of his truck, but I didn't. Something within me said: *Your name is also on that truck and you might go to jail. You have to keep it together for your children. If something happens to you, what will happen to them?*

Evidently I had not moved on, but my ex-husband wanted to prove to me that he had moved on with his life. It was then I knew I had to leave before someone really got hurt in this love/hate relationship.

Taking both children, I moved away from Texas to have peace of mind and to start over. I packed up and moved back to Oklahoma, where I supported both my children and myself without any support from my ex-husband and their father. In fact, he rarely spoke to the children or me when I would call him. Therefore, I stopped trying to communicate with him and began looking up to God and moved forward in life.

> ***Come near to God and He will come near to you…Humble yourselves before the Lord and He will lift you up.***
>
> ***(James 4:8, 10 NIV)***

Step V—Feelings of No Respect
To help guide you through the healing process of divorce, explain your situation:

What Happened?

_____

_____

_____

_____

_____

_____

_____

_____

_____

Divorce Hurts: He Doesn't Want Me as His Wife Anymore

Your Feelings at the time:

What would you do differently?

CHAPTER 6
Getting Another Chance

It always amazes me how good God is. I moved in with one of my aunts, and the first week there, I woke up and decided to start looking in the yellow pages for a job. I located the Oklahoma Department of Human Resources and called to see if they were hiring. The lady who answered the phone advised me that they did indeed need someone to work temporarily. She asked me a few questions and then told me to come in to discuss the job further, and I got it! Praise the Lord I was working!

Yet, my ultimate goal was to begin working again for the health insurance industry. Shortly afterward I did get the job I wanted, which was working with health insurance.

Not long after that, I met a wonderful guy who called and checked on me every day. He happened to be a big body buff. We had a great friendship, and he had the ability to motivate me and keep me in shape as well. Through this friendship I learned his brother was actually married to one of my cousins, so it seemed perfect.

My son was eight years old, and my daughter was four years old. Sadly, yet understandably, my son didn't take too well to this new man in my life because he felt he was the man of the house, and no one was going to get close to his mother.

Divorce Hurts: He Doesn't Want Me as His Wife Anymore

Our relationship started to go south from the day my ex-husband called. After about six months, he suddenly decided to visit. He also said we needed to accept each other's lives and be more involved with the children, together. I was so happy to hear from him that I offered him lodging with me if and when he came to visit. After I told my friend of my ex-husband's impending visit, he wasn't the same. He gave up on our relationship because he didn't agree with my ex-husband staying with me.

I guess my friend was right; it wasn't a good situation. When my ex-husband and I ended up seeing each other at that visit, we made love. That visit determined we still wanted to be together.

About the time he returned home to Texas, summer was near and the school year was just ending for our children. In our divorce agreement, we had decided I would keep them during the school year, and he would keep them during the summer. However, when the time came to pick up the children, we decided that I would move back with him too. I told him that if he was willing to arrange for everything, I would go. I gave my two-week notice and broke my apartment lease.

What a big mistake I made! Our reconciliation didn't last long at all, and soon afterward we found ourselves back at odds with each other and split up again. The day he moved out was the same day I was told he was with another woman (the one he left for me when we first met). How awful was that? The reason I found out is because he took a present from me that he had brought me for Christmas, and I went over to his apartment to get it. I was so very angry and emotionally unstable that he called the police on me. The police came and asked him if he had another female in the apartment with him. He told them the truth, and they asked him to just give me my Christmas present back so I would leave. "WOW." I always knew this woman was hanging around to have another chance with my husband by any means necessary. I wondered how long that relationship was going on behind my back. Now I think the only reason he wanted me to move back was to be a babysitter for our children that summer. If I had been thinking straight, I would at least have enjoyed the summer without the children and let him have full responsibility before rushing back.

My ex-husband was good at writing me letters because he never felt he could communicate his feelings to me either. This is a letter he wrote, which happened to be four-pages long. He wrote this one to me after I moved back from Oklahoma to Texas and we had split up again. I think it expresses his true feelings:

Man what a trip!!! What a total trip this has been. Ever since I first saw you at the Casa Amigo 'til this letter I'm writing, "WHAT A TRIP." Look, Dana, there's nothing for you to understand. You don't have to ask me or wonder what I wanted. I've always told you. I know that you are saying "Sex." As usual, you turned it into something else. I enjoyed your "Story," it was entertaining. The sad thing about this all is; Oh it's nothing but bad timing. Totally bad timing. When you were ready to be honest and in love, married, devoted, trusting, loving I was a child (15 yrs). When I was ready for those things you were a child (20 yrs). I cannot, for the life of me, change what's happened. The pain I caused you. The games I played. Oh, yes, I know the S.O.B. I was, I am well aware. Even if I tried to forget, I always had you to remind me.

Maybe you were confused back then but you had the "Star Football Player." As long as you had that it didn't really matter what I did, you wouldn't leave me for long. I knew it and maybe you did to. That's cool. That's the only reason you put up with the crap I dished out. Hey, baby, I was just doing what I was taught.

Finally, (thank you Jesus) I saw just what a- -hole I really was, but could I get you to believe me? I didn't know. Will you marry me? You said yes finally. That's when you had a real prince. Then, at that time, I truly became a man. You couldn't see that. Wasn't that always what you wanted from me? That's what you said anyway. You wanted honesty, you wanted me to stop having sex, dating and seeing other women behind your back. That's what I started with. Eventually, you were able to help me calm down, stop cursing so much, stop patting behinds and most importantly, not press you for attention. I didn't deserve attention because I was a liar and a cheat. At first that was okay. All I wanted was a chance, Dana, just one more solitary, small chance-. I guess I didn't deserve it. But I figured, hey, I've been such an S.O.B. to this lady I deserve this. Really I didn't. Every chance you had, you told me what a liar and sorry man I was. All you want is for men to take you out to be seen looking good. A virtual Mercedes Benz of a woman. That's cool. I don't need a good-looking woman to show off; I need a good-looking woman who's mine. I'm not interested in any other men you've had relations with, I don't care. Lord knows I've done my share. All I want is to live for today and believe in the future. I must have a lady who believes in the same thing.

Now you can go back to "looking good" only. Oh, I know I'm over weight. But you know something, Dana, so are you. Your body looks good but it's not the same body it was 15 yrs ago. But for me I feel the same about it. For you I'm just a fat lying stinky slob. I don't say that to be hateful, just truthful. That's okay, inside me there is beauty; you can't see it but you don't look to try to find it. I know sick people have felt on and abused you growing up. But, hey baby, never, I mean never, have I ever had anything but love and respect in my heart whenever I touched you. All I ever wanted was to make you feel good. When it was new to you I guess you did enjoy it. Now it's not so new, so it feels like molestation—very repulsive to you. So repulsive that not only don't you want to be touched, you don't want to touch. And oral sex—well, no need to comment on that.

Even the times I went out on a limb and told you things I didn't have to, it was just more ammunition for you to shoot at me. I'd always think, "This time she won't act like this." Wrong again. About the furniture in my apartment, I don't get what the deal is. I've told you a million times I wasn't seeing anyone, so you and I wouldn't be messing up trying to get back together. I didn't want to start our "new life" off by doing the same stupid stuff I did in the past. I know dear, I'm a liar and a cheat, a fat one at that. You take it as a slap (surprise) in the face. What a trip.

Yep, you do know about my past; I believe that's good. Always know though, what you had and what you have is two totally different things. Yep, you've slept around on me too. But I'm still the monster. You also lied and made mistakes but I'm still the monster. Go figure. You're right; I don't know you. I guess I never will. But I don't really think you know yourself. That's cool also. I'm praying for you. I can't give you what you need. You led me to believe I could satisfy you. In the process you'd take care of me. You'd rather wash dishes, cook, and clean than touch me. Now that makes a fella feel real wanted. I know about your problems and things, but I have things to deal with too. Does that matter? You say I'm "holding you back." Well, not anymore.

I am ashamed at how I treated you long ago. (Short while ago.) Whatever it seems like to you, I didn't have enough knowledge to know the deal then. I do now. It's really a shame you won't ever get to enjoy the happiness you deserve, a loving man like me.

All you'll ever think about is lies when you think of me. I hate that but I accept it. I don't deserve it though. So anyway, here we are now. Counting the days until we are finished forever. What a trip. Is it your PMS? Acting up? Who knows? I seldom know where the PMS ends and begins.

Look, sweetheart, I'm not trying to be vengeful, hateful or hurtful. (I know you don't buy that.) Although that's probably bull to you, I have to be honest from my heart. You can't and won't believe me, but at least for my part I'm being truthful. You speak of how much you gave up coming back down here. What exactly did you give up to leave Dallas?? The exact same thing—job, apartment and father of your children. You didn't have a job or money. But you have men. You came back here; you had love. You didn't have a job but you knew I'd take care of you. Don't you see? You just wanted me to help with the care of our children. You know with any other man, the things I do you would've had to give a lot more. You came down here and took a vacation. Didn't want to do anything for me or the kids. You know that wasn't right. But did I complain? I worked, cooked, cleaned, and washed dishes. See, you know I'm the only man that would tolerate that kind of crap. Just like you said, "I don't want a man," that's me included. Me on the other hand, I want a woman for love, for love-making, for companionship, for trust and to depend. With your men you couldn't let them do too much because they'd expect certain things. All you wanted was someone to give to you without you having to give anything back. I'm not that man. Whatever happened to your fellas? The fella you moved up there (Tulsa) to be with? Mr. Big

Money. Whatever happened to Mr. Fine Body? See, I used to believe if I had money and a fine body I could get you to love me. How wrong I was. You had those things and still weren't satisfied. You just won't give to a man.

This was the end of the letter.

Yes, I quit my job in Oklahoma to go back to my ex-husband in Texas, so I wasn't working. I also felt I deserved a vacation, after having the children by myself all those months with no support from him. And, if I hadn't moved back to be with him, he was supposed to keep the children for the summer anyway. I just thought I would let him experience not having any support, and I took a break even though I moved back in with him. And, I still believed we would be together forever. My ex-husband and I always wrote letters to each other, whether they were negative or positive feelings about our relationship.

It's rather sad, but after this letter my ex-husband wrote, we went our separate ways for a little while longer. I think all together we stayed apart less than two years before we tried re-marrying again.

Things were going good; we had found a church to start attending in Texas with a minister and his wife from our own hometown in Oklahoma. My ex-husband totally trusted our pastor and his wife, and we had started fellowshipping together and enjoying our new church family.

We soon knew it was time for us to get things right in the sight of God. We began marriage counseling with our pastor, and then we agreed to re-marry and make a new start. God was giving us another chance at marriage to get it right.

The day we decided to re-marry was May 22, 1994, approximately ten years after the first time we said, "I Do" in our marriage vows. We figured that in the sight of God, we really had never been divorced. With our re-marriage, we found ourselves back as husband and wife. I knew that this would be our "...till death do us part."

> *And now these three remain: faith, hope and love. But the greatest of these is love.*
>
> **(1 Corinthians 13:13 NIV)**

Praise God for His Mercy and Grace to give us another chance at marriage.

Step VI—Getting Another Chance
To help guide you through the healing process of divorce, explain your situation:

<u>What Happened?</u>
(Don't let pride get in the way)

_____

_____

_____

_____

_____

_____

_____

_____

_____

_____

Your Feelings at the time:
(Walking in faith)

What would you do differently?
(Obedience is better than sacrifice)

_____

_____

_____

_____

_____

_____

_____

_____

_____

_____

_____

_____

CHAPTER 7
Divorce Hurts

Our marriage lasted eleven more years, and during that time I tried very hard to please my husband. Also, during that time period, things were going well for us. My husband joined a church that had a minister and wife he trusted, and then he was soon baptized. It was the most precious thing that had ever happened in our family. He then became active in church by joining the men's choir, and he even attended Sunday school. Together we even headed up a ministry called "Couples in Christ." I was faithful to the sanctuary choir, and my sisterhood ministry spiritual life was great, and we both knew God was in the center holding us together.

Then came a surprise. My husband's best friend's brother showed up at the same church we were going to and started working in the youth ministry. This brought him back in the loop of our life again, which wasn't good. It was not long before my husband began getting involved again with his best friend's brother. That's when problems in our marriage began to surface again.

The best friend's brother had a high influence on my husband, whom my husband considered as a mentor and my husband respected a great deal, even more after the best friend's brother became a minister. I really don't know what exactly happened to us, but I do know that the best friend's brother started having problems in his third marriage, and we began having problems in ours about the same time.

It had gotten so bad in our relationship that Sunday mornings, when we got ready for church, was the best part of our week. Surprisingly, both of us looked forward to going to church, dressing up in our best attire and hearing the "Word of God" spoken from the pulpit. Yet sadly, when we got in the car each Sunday morning, we didn't have two words to say to each other all the way to church.

Upon arriving at the church, the car doors would open, and it was all smiles and saying, "Hi, Brother and Sister…" Oh, how we put up a good front—even to the point of being affectionate and attentive to each other during church service.

After we returned home, we would be two different people—almost to the point of roommates who didn't even like each other. It was as if we had nothing to say to or do for each other. Within the walls of our own home, we'd go our separate ways, watching two separate televisions and doing our own "thing," unless we had invited the minister and his wife or other family members over for Sunday dinner.

Most people and family thought we were the perfect couple—that we had gotten our act together and were on the right path in life and marriage.

As I look back, at the time my husband was doing well. He had gone from a warehouse job to a manager at a large telephone company. I supported his efforts to change jobs. At first it was a sacrifice financially, but we wanted better things for him and our family, and it paid off. We were able to build a big, beautiful two-story home, and have nice cars. My husband at the time even had a motorcycle to enjoy in his leisure time.

In my job at the health insurance corporation, I was being acknowledged, receiving rewards and traveling every other month. Things were the best they had ever been.

We were on borrowed time. Soon, our "wonderful life" was going to take another turn for the worse and talk of divorce faced us again. My husband's manhood problem started again. For answers, he began looking to his friends, especially his mentor because I just didn't know how to help him. Once this problem surfaced again, he didn't want to participate in any more church activities.

I thought it would be good if we joined the choir together and kept facilitating the Couples in Christ group—that didn't even work. So, again, I changed my life to fit with his. I began to let God down as well. First, I got out of the choir, thinking this would allow us to spend more time together. Next, we stopped doing Couples in Christ because this was his decision. Somehow I knew things would not be the same and that the old devil was again getting busy in our relationship.

* * *

During our second go at marriage, I decided to complete my education, and I did just that. First, I completed my undergraduate work, and then went on to get my master's degree. Having accomplished one of my goals in life, I was extremely happy and proud of myself. On the other hand, my husband felt he didn't need further education to succeed in life. Many times people are lucky, but most jobs require a degree of some sort.

Personally, I believed an education would help our family in the long run financially, and inspire our children to become college educated. Basically, I didn't want them to struggle through life as we had done. Like most parents, I wanted something better for them. My husband was disappointed that my decision to further my education was a big strain on our marriage, especially my decision to go back and complete my master's degree. He felt he had sacrificed and supported my efforts enough when I received my bachelor's degree but not the master's. I should have listened and respected him since he desperately needed my attention at home with him. The conflict in this part of our marriage should have been managed better, because it was necessary for both of us to be committed to the same goals and objectives.

* * *

This time when I realized things were deteriorating in my marriage, I immediately began to fast and pray. Soon it was obvious that, though I didn't want the devil to take my marriage again, this time my husband had given up the will to fight for our marriage.

One morning he just casually mentioned, "We should get a divorce."

Divorce Hurts: He Doesn't Want Me as His Wife Anymore

My immediate thought was: *Wow! What are you saying?* Looking back, I realized there had been changes in my husband that I had observed happening right before my eyes, but I had obviously ignored the signs. His clothes, cologne, and even his music had been changing. It seemed he was reverting to his younger years. What he wanted was to feel free to do what he pleased. Yet, we had all these bills and debt that took up most of our financial resources.

One thing I did manage to do was save enough money in order to help take care of my grandfather because he was elderly and needed support from the family. Many times I traveled between Texas and Oklahoma, helping as much as I could with his care. Usually I went by myself because my husband never, and I mean never, wanted to go with me.

On January 4, 2003, during one of my times of fasting and praying, I had a dream. I'm not sure how it works, but I feel certain that some dreams do have special meaning. Immediately, I awoke and wrote everything down before I forgot any of it.

The dream involved my family. My son, daughter, husband, and one of my uncles were traveling with me. It seemed I had been on this trip before, and there was only one way to get to our destination, and that was to take the "right" way, which I had taken the other time. But this time my husband was driving, and when he took a wrong turn, we were all headed the wrong way—with no traction for the car—it was just going straight down, falling, falling, falling straight down. Feeling destruction and accepting the end, my daughter started to get out, but her father pulled her back to save her or at least save her to stay inside the car. It was at that point when I began to pray and have faith that God would help us. Then a man appeared with a contract or agreement. He asked me if I wanted to take the right road—as if I could change things. All I had to do was say, "Yes," which I did. At that time I woke up.

In April 2003, my husband and I decided to separate within the confinement of our own home. We agreed that I'd move upstairs to the guest room. We agreed this seemed to be the best solution for us at that point in our marriage. Based on our communication with each other, we both realized we were very frustrated and dealing with high emotions and feelings. But, I must say, for the first time in our marriage, we were able to see through each other's eyes and truly were able to understand the meaning of it all. I have to give God, my Father, the glory because through three months of fasting and praying, God prepared me to survive this madness we called a marriage.

My husband truly is an outstanding man, and I believe he still has true love for me. I just don't think he understood the expectations and pressure I was feeling in trying to please his physical and emotional needs.

This behavior would go on for about two more years as we struggled with our marriage. Often I would go from "our" bedroom to the upstairs bedroom. Probably that lasted another year of our marriage. We didn't even have sex although we tried on several occasions; it was all about his manhood again, not being able to perform. But I always got the blame for not being affectionate, loving, or caring toward him. He told me he even felt I was undermining him when it came to our children as well. Truly, I really didn't understand his behavior at all.

The devil's grip had crept into our lives again as my husband started hanging around with his best friend's brother. Before I knew it, we were arguing about divorcing again. All I knew was that I didn't want a divorce—I'd rather be separated. I, in no way, wanted a divorce. Separation, to me, was the only option for us until we made our way back to each other. My husband had a different viewpoint. It had to be divorce, and he was not willing to go through a separation. But, lo and behold, I soon found out his best friend's brother (the good reverend) was also having marital problems, and he ended up helping my husband complete divorce papers "again." This happened right after my husband asked if this man could give us marriage counseling. I knew it was not in our best interest, but I wanted to make my husband happy and agreed to the counseling sessions with (the good reverend). Why a man of God would help someone, especially another man, get a divorce?

> ***Therefore what God has joined together, let man not separate.***
>
> **(Mark 10:9 NIV)**

My soon-to-be ex-husband brought the divorce papers home, wanting my signature. He handed me the divorce papers and casually asked me to sign them. My response was, "And if I don't?"

Immediately he went into a tirade saying, "I spent the money to file for the divorce!"

Since he had an attitude suggesting he knew I might not sign them, I left the house and didn't sign them at that time. My first feelings were that I was angry and insulted that he had had the nerve to give me the divorce papers in the first place. Getting in my car, I drove to the nearby grocery store, where I called my dad and cried my heart out to him. There was such an awful pain inside of me as I thought of losing my husband and separating my family again. But remembering the look in my husband's eyes, I knew his heart did not belong to me anymore. His actions were so very cold and indifferent towards me.

In looking back, I see the signs were there, but I must have been in denial, even when he asked me to separate our checking accounts and the cell phone bill, and to take me off his health insurance policy. Yet I had failed to see what was coming. I never allowed myself to even contemplate the idea of our getting a divorce.

Giving him a divorce would be the hardest thing I had ever done. Naturally emotional, I cried a lot and felt deceived and betrayed. As it had been earlier in our marriage, it was all about my husband and his best friend's brother, who would soon divorce his wife as well. The two men planned to move in together in order to help each other financially.

Wow, who was going to help me financially! My feelings were the last thing on his list; even his friends came before me. Soon I realized he would lie or cover up incidents just to save his back or any of his best friend's.

All I wanted was for my ex-husband to lay down his life for me, his wife. But, he didn't care about our relationship, and he started taking off his wedding ring before our divorce was even final. If he could, he just wanted to walk off and leave our home, and it was just another repeat of our last divorce. I knew that God's original purpose for marriage was that the union should not be broken, yet we were failing again.

Life did not prepare me for the outcome of my choices I had made, and sometimes I made drastic decisions—just so my husband would notice me and seem to care.

When my husband and I were divorced for the second time, it caused me to feel as if I had been treated unfairly and very unappreciated. The divorce was extremely difficult for me. It left me hurt, and the pain was as if someone had ripped out my heart and left me on the side looking at it and feeling helpless. All I could do is wait and hope my heart would stop beating so I could rest from the emptiness I felt inside. I really began to understand the full meaning of Mark 10:8 that says, *"And the two shall become one flesh; so then they are no longer two, but one flesh."* Suddenly half of me was now missing, and I was not a whole person inside without my husband and best friend.

> *Greater love has no one than this,*
> *that he lay down his life for his friends.*
>
> **(John 15:13 NIV)**

Step VII—Divorce Hurts

To help guide you through the healing process of divorce, explain your situation:

What Happened?

_____

_____

_____

_____

_____

_____

_____

_____

_____

_____

Divorce Hurts: He Doesn't Want Me as His Wife Anymore

Your Feelings at the time:

What would you do differently?

CHAPTER 8
Grief Stages

The first stage of my divorce I spent denying that my husband would actually have the nerve to divorce me. Even when I signed the divorce papers, I still honestly believed in my heart that he would not submit them to the court or go through with it. After he sent me the papers and went to court in my behalf, I still did not believe it was what he wanted. I had been with this man since I was fourteen—more than half my life, and we had always found our way back to one another.

Most of our problems stemmed from our pride to yield to the other, and I looked at the divorce as we had gone further than I expected. My now ex-husband moved on very quickly with his life, but I clung securely to the belief he would open his heart and let me back in again—it never happened. He had begun a serious relationship, supposedly less than six months after our divorce, and then he moved in with the woman. When mentioning her to me, he described her as "my girl." What a shock! I was not prepared to ever hear anything like that in my life! Looking back, I realize that even then I still hoped he would see the good in our marriage and tell me it was all a big mistake and come back to me. I was definitely in denial.

One of the biggest reasons I attribute to my denial is that I clung to the belief in what my ex-husband had always told me—that we were forever, as he stated in one of his love letters to me:

Dana,

It has been many years since I've written you a love letter. Way too many years. I want you to know that I'm more in love with you every minute we've traveled so many miles together; I don't ever want to be without you. Alone. That's what I'd be without you. Oh, I could probably find a girlfriend, or something along those lines, but I could only be happy with you. I know I bitch and whine sometimes but it's not because I'm upset because you don't work. It's mainly because every penny (almost) I make we pay bills. There are so many things I want to give you. Things a good mother and loving wife deserves. All I have or ever had was just my love. I hope that my love will be enough to make you hang around 'til I can give you all the extras you deserve. We've come a long way since the 9th grade. But, I truly, truly believe that the best, by far, is yet to come. Keep your chin up and be proud of yourself. I AM!! Your husband (4-ever).

This was the end of the letter.

Our love was like a roller coaster ride; sometimes we were up, and sometimes we were down but always moving fast. I just always believed I would be his "Muffin," or his "Lovely Bride" forever.

* * *

During the second stage of the divorce, I was shocked at the unfeeling rejection from my ex-husband. It was as though I didn't even know this person. He treated me as if I was a stranger, and I really didn't understand his behavior. Whenever I called him, I automatically and subconsciously expected the happy, understanding guy to whom I had been married. Instead, I received the cold shoulder. Then I noticed whenever I called that my calls were not important enough for him to answer. He let the answer machine take my message and then he might call me days later. When we did talk, he called me by my first name (Dana). I felt so out of place in his life, in my family's life, and in his family's life. Everything seemed so awkward to me. I didn't know how to act or react to his attitudes as he made it painfully clear I was shut out of his life or his plans. There was no love or affection that I could glean at all from this man. In my mind I kept asking: *What happened to the godly man I married (second time around)? He would never talk or treat me in this manner.*

* * *

It was in the third stage following the divorce that my ex-husband had the nerve to tell me, "You had your chance, and you need to move on." Now, how cruel was that?

After that I got very angry with him. It was like loving someone and wanting to treat them right, but at the same time, the pain inside is so deep it overwhelms your senses.

At that stage it is very, very hard to even want to be kind. My first instincts were to lash out at him, but what was the use when he had made it clear he really didn't care or wasn't interested in my feelings at that point? What kept going around in my head was the idea that he should have tried harder and done more to try and keep his family together and his wife happy.

Adding fuel to the fire was that whenever he talked with me, he seemed so cool and collected, not upset at all that his family was now torn apart. It hurt that he obviously could move on and not think twice about all the history and love we had shared in our lifetime together. Basically, I just didn't understand how he could talk and act so indifferently towards me...maybe because he did not want to fight with me. However, it left me feeling so helpless in my efforts to keep it all together.

The last straw was his decision to get married and move with this woman back to Oklahoma. To my way of thinking at the time, it was an insult to me—how humiliating. Of course I kept asking myself: *How could he take someone else to our hometown? How could he do everything with her that we had talked about doing together? I am so angry. Why would he leave me after we had raised our children?* When he left, our daughter had just graduated from high school.

Awful thoughts kept going through my mind. One was: *Did he just hold on until the children were reared and then had planned to leave me so he could live the life of his dreams? Had he deliberately planned to leave me in the cold to start over with no one and nothing?*

The fourth part of my processing was when I began to bargain with my ex-husband. It was important, at the time, for me to let him know how I felt and how badly he had hurt me. When I received an overpayment check in the mail for our house insurance, it had both our names on it. I decided to ask him to have lunch and then give him some of the money.

My ex-husband agreed to have lunch with me, and when we met, I wasted no time in telling him, "In God's eyes you are still my husband, and I don't believe you would actually marry someone else. If you did, it would be letting the devil have his way, and then he would have defeated us and destroyed our marriage."

When I finished, my ex-husband sat there at a loss for words, not knowing what to say. Since he was speechless, I told him, "You don't have to say anything. In our first divorce, I asked you to come back to me but not this time. I need to know you love me enough to come back on your own."

Seeing his reaction it then hit me: His love for me at that particular time wasn't from God! He wanted to prove he could move on without me...and he did just that.

* * *

After that I went into a deep turmoil of depression. I sought help from those who didn't know either of us. What I wanted and needed were answers. It was important for me to know

Divorce Hurts: He Doesn't Want Me as His Wife Anymore

if I was the real reason my husband divorced me.

My first talk was with a Christian counselor, and she could find nothing wrong with me. She felt, after hearing my side of the story, that my ex-husband was selfish and very childish for leaving. It was hard for this counselor to understand why I would even want this man back considering all our past history—the first divorce, his moving on so quickly, moving in with another woman, and then callously letting me know he was going to get married. This counselor felt I deserved so much more to be happy.

Even after those counseling sessions, I really tried my hardest to look forward and let it all go. I was doing pretty well until I found out my ex-husband was up in Texas moving all his stuff and this woman back to our hometown. What really hurt was that some of our friends and his family came to help support this effort. That was when I hit rock bottom and could not control my emotions any longer. I gave up on everything including my job. Depression took over, and my body shut down. It seemed all I did was cry and cry. Soon, I got to the point where I didn't want to face the days ahead.

When I finally became physically sick and had to go to the doctor, his initial diagnosis, just listening to me ramble on and on, was that I probably was having a nervous breakdown. One thing for sure is that I was very depressed and had serious anxiety problems. I felt so horrible inside; my mind, body, and soul had been drained of all energy and will.

Divorce Hurts: He Doesn't Want Me as His Wife Anymore

In order to overcome my "hardship," it became necessary for me to finally take the heat and accept my ex-husband's behavior and the fact that we were truly divorced. It was also necessary for me to accept my part of the blame. As I heard the many reasons my ex-husband gave to others, and me, it became very apparent that he felt the divorce was my fault! He actually blamed me for not being the wife he needed nor wanted at this time in his life! It was hard for me to accept what he said about things he felt were wrong with me as an affectionate and submissive wife. I call it the "just blame me" when someone has to take the heat for all the wrongs. In our marriage it was me. Therefore, I took full responsibility for my lack of affection, my non-submissive ways, and whatever other reasons my ex-husband gave for not wanting me to be his wife any longer.

I had truly wanted to be affectionate and submissive to my husband, but the reality is a husband has to serve his wife lovingly whether she is submissive or not. A wife is to be obedient and submissive whether or not her husband is showing her Christ-like love, and this is where I failed. The idea of being submissive to a man who was negligent, careless, and irresponsible with my heart left me experiencing feelings of resentment, fear, and anger. Of course I was frustrated with my efforts because of the thought of committing myself to his care and judgment. The long and short of it is that I just could not trust him to do the right thing by me, especially when I saw everything from a significantly different point of view. *A married woman is as responsible to follow her husband, as her husband is responsible to follow the Lord.*

> **Submit to one another out of reverence for Christ. Wives submit to your husbands as to the Lord. For the husband is the head of the wife as Christ is the head of the church…..Husbands, love your wives, just as Christ loved the church and gave himself up for her to make her holy, cleansing her by the washing with water through the word,…….However, each one of you also must love his wife as he loves himself, and the wife must respect her husband.**
>
> **(Ephesians 5:21-33 NIV)**

I have no trouble accepting that my ex-husband and I are two imperfect people, who hurt and misled one another. We both helped make a mess of things. I guess what I wanted was for my ex-husband to make it right after I had told him of my deep hurt and displeasure with our mistakes. Since we both were accountable to God and a husband's first responsibility is to remain true to the Lord, I did not want a divorce. What I wanted was for my ex-husband to save us through the hope and faith of our Lord and Savior, Jesus Christ!

The Virtuous Woman (Proverbs 31:10-31)

(RBC – What does God Expect of a Woman)

Here are some key points to remember from this text. A commendable wife and mother lives for her home and family:

Is industrious

Self-disciplined and orderly

Is a sharp business woman

Has good, refined tastes

Manifests the grace of hospitality

Charitable in time of need

Spiritually minded

Be mindful of the qualities of the "Virtuous woman" in Proverbs 31. We may feel some of these areas are lacking, but God understands, yet expects us, with His help, to have godly attitudes in each area.

Step VIII—Grief Stages

To help guide you through the healing process of divorce, explain your situation:

What Happened?

_____

_____

_____

_____

_____

_____

_____

_____

_____

Your Feelings at the time:

Divorce Hurts: He Doesn't Want Me as His Wife Anymore

What would you do differently?

CHAPTER 9
Restoration and Healing

After much praying and struggling, I finally realized and accepted that no matter what happens, my life and future were in God's hands. So, to restore my mind, body, and soul, I began my healing process by not worrying about what my ex-husband was saying, doing, and with whom he was doing it. I had to trust in the Bible verse that says, *"If God is for me, who can be against me?"* It was important for me to realize the battle was not mine to fight. Finally, I reached the point where I was able to give it all to the Lord. Then I relaxed and let God deal with my depression and anxiety.

To help guide me through the process, God, my Father, rescued me from myself, restored my broken relationships, and righted the wrongs in my life. I had to know that God was going to restore and provide for me. That He was going to love me, no matter what.

God was and should have always been my first love. All my passion and faith should have been for my Savior. Whatever happened in my life, whether good or bad, I should never have stopped loving and praising the Lord for his goodness and mercy.

> *Nevertheless I have this against you, that you have left your first love.*
> **(Revelation 2:4 NKJV)**

It was then time for me to thank God for renewing my attitude and spirit. I had to give up my old thoughts and habits to Him and embrace a new path of life for myself. In other words, I had to come out of me and realize it's not about me at all. It's all about God and His will for my life!

My ex-husband was the man God intended to be my husband to love, to have, and to hold me for a lifetime—the man that would lay down his very life to spend with me. Yet, I question if my ex-husband was an illusion or a fantasy of a husband because he would not have treated me as he did if he had been my mate for a lifetime, to cherish me with all his heart. Bottom line, my ex-husband had a level of insecurities with me that is hard to describe—except, he wanted to experience a different life with another wife. I believe God allowed our marriage to end due to our pride and giving up on each other which helped the devil to destroy our marriage. We needed to continue to have the Faith that God was going to work it out no matter how bad the situation seemed...we were God's children.

Statistically, **50% of all marriages in America end in divorce**, according to divocerate.org. This data is reasonably close to actual. The Americans for Divorce Reform estimates that "probably 40 or possibly even 50 percent of marriages will end in divorce if current trends continue." which is actually a projection. The divorce rate in America for first marriage vs. second or third marriage: 50% percent of first marriages, 67% of second, and 74% of third marriages end in divorce, according to Jennifer Baker of the Forest Institute of Professional Psychology in Springfield, Missouri. The divorce rate in America for childless couples and couples with children according to the Discovery Channel: couples with children have a slightly lower rate of divorce than childless couples. Sociologists believe that childlessness is also a common cause of divorce. The absence of children leads to loneliness and weariness and even in the United States at least 66 percent of all divorced couples are childless. I heard that one out of every four marriages will deal with infidelity. Also, I heard the topic on one of my favorite talk shows, "Oprah," on how divorce is rapid. What is happening to our families? Especially the increasing number of Christians whose marriages fall into this category saddens me. If you choose to get married and say, "I do," mean it! We must take a stand to be committed in marriage—one woman/one man for a lifetime. *Don't Give Up!*

* * *

Soon, it was time for me to start making decisions that were good and release the bondage from my past. I needed to understand who I was and my feelings, to be happy, to like the person within me, and to learn my strengths and my weaknesses. Now I understood that my ex-husband was the only man I had known to love, and that is why I kept repeating what I had learned. Now it was about walking more in truth and not in lies, which I had been doing for years while wanting this man to love me, to be my best friend, to care about my feelings, and to understand the things that made me happy. I didn't want things done for me out of obligation, but because he truly wanted to do them or enjoyed doing them. It wasn't for him to change for me, and that's what made him so frustrated. I just desired to feel truly loved by him, not him trying so hard it seemed unreal and not natural. Therefore both of us and the children struggled through our unhappiness.

It took time, but now I have learned to trust the Lord for all my needs. I will delight in the fact I know about the love of God. I will commit my life, family, job, and possessions to His control and guidance. Anything that has been promised to me, I know God shall bring it to pass and whatever I'm bold enough to trust Him with, He will deliver. So, forget about what's happened; don't keep going over old history. Be alert, be present. God is about to do something brand-new. Get ready, it's bursting out! Don't you see it? There it is!

> *Behold, I will do a new thing, now it shall spring forth; shall you not know it?*
> *I will even make a road in the wilderness and rivers in the desert.*
>
> **(Isaiah 43:19 NIV)**

In accepting God's promise, the key for me was to study God's word, understand His word, to pray without ceasing, and to truly believe that all things work together for good to those who love the Lord. Good can come out of the severe trials of life.

Being human, I sometimes ask God why I have to go through so many trials as a Christian. Over time I have come to believe the answer is that *there's a war going on for our very souls, and Christians need to know where to go in time of storms.* Trials bring patience and trust in the Lord. As a Christian I went through a growth pattern, so never reach the point where you can't trust anybody. Expect temptation because Jesus was also tempted. We must saturate our minds with the literature of the Bible and know scriptures. Don't sin against God and you won't sin against man. Prevention is the best method. Use wisdom from the Lord to let go, and let God lead, plan, and show you the purpose for your life—then proceed positively in prayer by faith.

Step IX—Restoration and Healing

To help guide you through the healing process of divorce, explain your future steps to be restored and healed:

<u>How can you be restored?</u>

_____

_____

_____

_____

_____

_____

_____

_____

_____

_____

How will you change your feelings?

_____

_____

_____

_____

_____

_____

_____

_____

_____

_____

_____

What are your steps to begin a healing process?

Testimony

I had known my ex-husband for many years. We had worked for the same company during our high school years. The summer of my junior year in college, he asked me out on a date. I had never been on a date, so this was a very big deal for me. It was love at first sight, and we were engaged four months later.

We had been married for about eighteen years when he came home the day before my birthday to tell me that he didn't want to be married any more. He also told me that I did nothing wrong, and it was not my fault. I will never forget that moment. I was standing in the kitchen. I remember falling to the floor in shock. He took my life, as I knew it, away from me that day. I knew in my heart that my marriage would never end, but it did.

I began to abuse prescription drugs with alcohol. I tried to commit suicide two times and spent a week in a psychiatric hospital. The day after my first attempt at suicide, I went into the living room to lie down on the couch. I had just dosed off when I felt someone sit down beside me and rub my back. To my surprise, there was no one sitting there. I am a religious person, and I believe someone (God) was letting me know that things would be okay. And with the support of my family and friends who I owe my life to, I recovered.

A divorce is never easy. Mine was a long and very bumpy road, but I survived everything that came my way. I have been

Divorce Hurts: He Doesn't Want Me as His Wife Anymore

divorced for several years, and it has not been easy starting over, but I did it. I am looking forward to my future.

Denise Ellis

CHAPTER 10
Deliverance from Troubles

It was important for me to think straight about my troubles and the reason for them. The troubles I experienced came in all sizes and shapes, which affected my health, career and relationships with others.

As I grew, the Lord helped me realize that my ex-husband, wishing for the "good old days" when times were easy and life was fun, had caused a good deal of my unhappiness. Being human, I have to admit to wishing things were still that easy and simple; but now I am more realistic. Looking back upon my fading memories, I now realize that when I was younger, I enjoyed any situation just to be near my ex-husband. Yet, as it happens in life, the happiness changed and was taken away from us by real-life situations. It took some time, but now I understand this world and everything in it is unstable and unpredictable. When my marriage ended, I had been left longing for something or someone that lasted forever. The truth is the only thing I really had was God's word that, *"...righteousness endures forever."* (Psalm 112: 9). It is the only thing that is untouched and unharmed by time and worldly circumstances. This is the one sure thing that nothing in the world can take away from you. Life is not always fair, but God is always faithful.

* * *

The Lord impressed upon me that in order to be delivered

from my troubles, it was important for me to forgive my ex-husband and his best friend's brother (the good reverend). For me to do this, I needed to repent and gain the trust and dignity I had once lost.

For a time I felt so unworthy to even hold my head up in the presence of my family, friends, and especially my church family. You see, my ex-husband and I had been the lead facilitators of the couples ministry at our church for several years. I felt we should have been able to discern what was best for our marriage to grow stronger. Our love, knowledge and spiritual growth should have endured the test based on the principles of the ministry. The ministry was created to help build and strengthen the family and keep couples together, helping them endure the challenges of being married. At the time, we were the married couple that had experienced and survived so many situations couples could experience, yet at the time, we were still together. And, if we could survive the obstacles in our marriage, anyone with prayer would survive. The whole point of the couple's ministry was to focus on the power of prayer to save your wife or husband from the wiles of the devil and stay focused on being supportive and committed to your spouse and family.

But, now, who could or would trust or believe in marriage after we let so many couples down that thought our marriage was strong enough to weather life's storms?

Back then I had accepted my life and thought everything was in order. Because of that, God had blessed me. Now much of it was all gone. I questioned God: *Why? Why me, Lord? Why so much pain? Why so much humility in my life?* I was a faithful servant. I did what was expected and tried to live by the Word and my question was still, *"Why? Why did my husband want to follow his best friend's brother and his friends over his wife?"* My only thought was: *"God please, look at me and help me! I'm all alone and in big trouble!"*

> **Turn to me and be gracious to me, for I am lonely and afflicted.**
> **The troubles of my heart have multiplied; free me from my anguish.**
>
> **(Psalm 25:16-17 NIV)**

Then, when I read Psalm 27, in these words God helped me realize that I still had much to learn and He had to take me through the storms, trials and tribulations. The experiences of hurt and pain would mold me into a better person to meet His purpose and will for my life. Upon understanding this point, I began to thank God for letting me experience my marriage, husband, two wonderful children, and the many blessings during that time.

Also, I realized that true love does not change with circumstances, and this is the kind of love that should be illustrated at all times in a Christian marriage. Christians should know that many changes are inevitable for married couples during their lifetime together, including health problems and growing older throughout the years. That's why it's important to believe and nurture the true biblical love that neither falters nor fails in spite of the differences or alterations that may come in a marriage.

One of the easiest and simplest reasons to walk away from a marriage or to get a divorce is incompatibility. If that is the case, everyone would be divorced because differences will surely come your way as it did in my marriage.

I had to "Get Up" and survive the awful devastation from my divorce and everything that followed. It took all my strength to overcome my hardship and, according to the Bible, to count it all joy.

> ***My brethren, count it all joy when you fall into various trials.***
>
> **(James 1:2 NKJV)**

Step X—Deliverance from Troubles

To help guide you through the healing process of divorce, explain your steps to move forward:

<u>Make a list of your trials</u>

_____

_____

_____

_____

_____

_____

_____

_____

_____

How will you grow from the troubles?

What step can you take forward?

CHAPTER 11
Finding Joy, Peace and Happiness

Because of everything that has happened in my life, I truly believe I now am a better person. I know my sins, and I've learned from my mistakes. Now, I am trusting and dependent on the Lord to instruct and guard my heart and guide my footsteps. God has given me a vision, a purpose to fulfill, and brought people and blessings into my life that I don't understand right now, but I'm leaning on His promises. It hasn't been easy, but I have learned not to lean on my own understanding, but trust in the Lord. True peace and joy I have found that humbles and satisfies all things within my grateful heart.

One thing I have learned is that God fashioned me to share my experiences on earth with others. He has given me His holiness, strength, purity, love, protection, and support. God helped me realize that I was special to Him, even if my ex-husband or anyone else didn't think so. My life is not to please people but to please God and be a faithful servant. I ask God not to let my life be dictated by what others think of me but what is pleasing to the Lord. I had to learn, it's not about the approval of men; it's that I must focus on serving the Lord and being about HIS business.

> *Am I now trying to win the approval of men, or of God? Or am I trying to please men? If I were still trying to please men,*
> *I would not be a servant of Christ.*
>
> **(Galatians 1:10 NIV)**

* * *

As I look back at my marriage, failures, and disappointments, I think about how God helped me repair my life. The answer is one day at a time; being thankful for waking up in the morning; looking at God's creation, the grass, the trees; and listening to the birds sing. I had to let go of the illusion my marriage still existed and accept the fact that my ex-husband had found a new wife to love and support. What had to happen was for me to take my attention off my ex-husband and his new wife and focus on God.

The toughest part of some days was if my ex-husband called, or I called him. It was as if we both knew in our hearts that we would always love each other. Yet, I didn't know what to expect or how to act now that there was another Mrs. X for him to call his own.

Knowing he had remarried helped me to stop wanting and waiting for him to call me so that I could hold onto his last loving and supporting words of kindness. It is hard to admit I had a harder time moving on than he did. Yes, I do say it! Frankly, it was harder than I expected because I truly loved him unconditionally, with a love that came from the depth of my soul. The hard part was not wishing he would feel the same way or understand so that things would get better for us.

The only place I could get some peace was when I stayed in God's word and prayed. It was amazing how God spoke to me through His holy word time and time again. He led me right to a passage or scripture I needed at the time. I knew it was His mercy and grace that directed my path.

* * *

Since my feelings and affections were still attached to my ex-husband, it was very hard for me to even think about having another relationship with a man. I'd sit on the couch day in and day out, thinking my life would be miserable without my high school sweetheart. I was convinced he was the only man for me and fixated on the fact I wanted things to work out so I could be with him for a lifetime.

In the midst of all my hurt, it was my son and daughter who shined the most in my life. They were such a source of strength, holding me up during my darkest hours of the day and night, letting me know I was a great mother and role model to them. My daughter told me she had always thought I was a strong and confident woman, and she wanted to be just like me, whereas my son said he just wanted nothing but happiness for me. Wow! Just those words let me know how very blessed I was to know I had reared my children to the best of my ability with much love and spiritual guidance.

Divorce Hurts: He Doesn't Want Me as His Wife Anymore

Now, both were servants helping their mother get through the hurt and pain from a broken heart and divorce.

I know the divorce was not easy for either of them. During that time, I was their rock until I wore down, becoming too weak to stand alone. Just at that time, do you know what happened? I thought I'd never find anyone to love me just for myself or understand what I was feeling...how could they understand? Having exhausted myself, my family, my mom, dad, sister and brother, pastor and wife, there was no one left with energy left to keep listening to me about how I felt and how I was hurting and what was I going to do. To everyone else it seemed so simple: Stop talking to my ex-husband and move on! Just move on! Just do it! Though I wanted it to be simple as that, it wasn't—no, not for me.

When I thought there was no one else to listen to my tears of pain, God rescued me and brought a kind and sweet young man into my life who offered support and friendship through the hurt and pain with which I was dealing. I really felt God had sent me a "Ram in the Bush" because he had to be a sacrifice for my hurt and pain. This young man was a strong, spiritual, kind, and loving man.

"Amazing grace how sweet the sound that saved a wretch like me..." There is so much power in the words of that song. Now, I sing when the devil wants to take my thoughts and focus on what I lost instead of all the blessings I have, beginning with my life. Now I have joy and peace that my God has shared with me through His scripture.

When I asked God if I should have a man move in with me to fulfill my needs and marry me, God answered me with this text:

> *For your Maker is your husband - the Lord Almighty is his name - the Holy One of Israel is your Redeemer; he is called the God of all the earth. The Lord will call you back as if you were a wife deserted and distressed in spirit - a wife who married young only to be rejected, says your God.*
>
> **(Isaiah 54:5-6 NIV)**

That sent chills through my soul. This scripture truly ministered to me because I was deserted, distressed, married young, and rejected. God let me know everything was going to be all right, and I could have joy, peace, and happiness knowing that the Lord was taking care of me as my husband. It is with surety that I know God is with me every step of the way, and He will never leave me nor forsake me if I just keep my mind, heart, and soul focused on Him. I have the assurance and hope in a brighter future.

When you fall, God will send an angel to support you, meaning there could be a person or several people who might come to help you get past the hurt and pain. You are a precious flower, and like all beautiful things, sometimes you have to go through a little dirt to grow. Let your beauty blossom into full bloom. You are a gift from God! When you find peace, you are in a position of control and power! Let go of all those negative emotions and allow God to heal and restore to you everything you have lost. Let a greater spirit of truth be your guide. Ask God to give you the patience to allow His plan for your life to be revealed. It is important to let the Holy Spirit guide you so that you will faithfully endure until you are put back together again and everything is in place for your life.

> *However, when He, the Spirit of truth, has come, He will guide you into all truth; for He will not speak on His own authority, but whatever He hears He will speak; and He will tell you things to come.*
>
> **(John 16:13 NIV)**

Step XI—Finding Joy, Peace, and Happiness

To help guide you through the healing process of divorce, explain your steps to move forward:

What are your steps to finding joy, peace and happiness?

_____

_____

_____

_____

_____

_____

_____

_____

_____

What are your steps in loving yourself?

What are your steps to meditate, read and pray?

CHAPTER 12
It's a New Day

Now it is time to move forward in your life and begin a new chapter. To do this you have to look at all the positives in your life and stop looking at the negatives. Be thankful for your life, health, mind, family, friends, job, and your abilities. I could go on and on with the endless blessings that we take for granted. Learn to celebrate your disappointments; thank God for His grace and love. Life is precious and too short to let the devil deceive us into thinking we are unworthy to be loved. We can have a peace of mind, knowing God will never leave us in despair. Don't worry; just let it go!

> *Therefore do not worry about tomorrow, for tomorrow will worry about itself. Each day has enough trouble of its own.*
>
> **(Matthew 6:34 NIV)**

We need to focus on some of the fruits of the Spirit. As Christians, we all have them. It's a decision, a choice to bring them out, and to be the best that we can be. These fruits will help guide you through each new day!

Our first fruit is **Love**. We need to show love because God is love. Love comes in all forms and stages; you will know when true love comes your way. Pray for God's unconditional love to surround you with His thoughts and His ways to live a godly life of love and support in order to heal you completely from your past. It is time to close the door on your past and open the one in front of you. That is where you will find a new beginning. Look ahead and don't look back. Let the past go completely and experience true love.

> *Love is patient. Love is kind. It does not envy, it does not boast, it is not proud. It is not rude, it is not self-seeking, it is not easily angered, and it keeps no record of wrongs. Love does not delight in evil but rejoices with the truth. It always protects, always trusts, always hopes, and always perseveres.*
>
> **(Corinthians 13: 4-7 NIV)**

Be patient. We want things fast and in a hurry. **Patience** is a fruit of the Spirit. Don't rush into something that you haven't prayed about or have not asked God's guidance to lead you all the way through. Ask Him for His mercy and protection to guard you from bad decisions or from your enemies. Let God fight your battles. Just pray for the ones that have hurt you or have spitefully used you. God has your back; He loves you. Be assured that God has heard your cry, and He will make the right decisions on your behalf. Whatever you do, do it God's way.

> *Away from me, all you who do evil, for the Lord has heard my weeping.*
> *The Lord has heard my cry for mercy; the Lord accepts my prayer.*
>
> **(Psalm 6:8-9 NIV)**

If you trust God, it will require some **Self-Control** on your part to live a life full of holiness. This fruit of the Spirit requires us to examine ourselves and learn not to be frustrated about our situation or with the disappointments and failures in life. I'm sure we all have things in our past that we regret; it's critical to our well-being to turn it over to God, to let Him take the guilt away through His grace and replace it with joy. If we are impatient, it is only a reflection of our own selfish, self-centered ways in which we handle the pressures in our life. When we learn to be patient, it is also an example of our love for others. Trust God!

> *Trust in the Lord with all your heart*
> *and lean not on your own understanding;*
> *in all your ways acknowledge him,*
> *and he will make your paths straight.*
>
> **(Proverbs 3:5-6 NIV)**

It's important to let Jesus be our model in all we say and do. This will show our own strength even in frustrating and difficult situations.

I recall many times when my ex-husband treated me rudely and without regard. At the time I didn't realize why. As for myself, I couldn't treat him mean and curse him out and act crazy, as I probably would have in the past. God had impressed me not to act in this manner. At the time, I couldn't explain my kind attitude towards him. All I could do was shut down and cry my eyes out each time he hurt my feelings or behaved in a manner that I didn't understand. After that, I would just pray for the suffering to go away. In my mind was the idea that I loved him with a godly love and didn't know how to get him to see the true love within me for him. Now, I better understand my actions and attitude. It is best to be patient and let God work it out for me.

Finally, move forward with bold persistence. This Fruit of the Spirit is **Faithfulness**. When you pray, something definitely happens. Keep pushing forward in spite of all the obstacles we have to climb such as loneliness, difficulties, desperation, rejection, hurt, pain, and even depression. Don't give up! Keep asking, keep looking, keep knocking, and soon you'll find the grace and mercy to overcome the trials of life. God wants us to be real. He knows our ways and our hearts; we can't hide the truth from God. The devil would sometimes have you believe it is your fault the way things happen and tries to make you feel ashamed of your sinful acts. He would have your mate or loved one come up with all kinds of excuses and maybe even have a long list, blaming you for what has happened in the marriage or your relationship.

The realization of life is that we are all sinful and made of the flesh. When this type of behavior happens, it is only used to make the accuser look good in his or her own eyes or look good to other people as if they can offer you something better than you have to offer them or they deserve something much better than your love for them. God so loved the world that He gave his only begotten son. You married a person for life, yet you want much more. You promised to love this person forever. A man should love his wife as God loved the church, but so often people don't live up to the marriage vows. This is called a form of deception, and God said their words sounded as if they honored God, but their hearts told another story—they are far from Him. (Matthew 15: 5-8)

The fact is, divorce hurts, and we must overcome the hurt and pain and accept that he or she does not want you to be his wife or her husband anymore. Be faithful and trust in the word of God to guide your footsteps in order to help deal with the hurt. Pray without despair. Faith moves us to believe and hope with a certainty that a new future will be provided with "His holy blessings."

Never let someone have so much control over your life that you lose the power of self-control and self-determination because this will mean someone has defeated you and taken control of your life, or so it may seem. Don't let the devil deceive you so that you are faking your faithful walk with Christ. The truth is that God has already given us the victory over the devil, this world and our flesh, but we must APPLY that victory to the circumstances of our life experiences on a daily basis and take a stand. **It is time for a change and God's people need to get back to the basics of Christian**

Living! Allow God to control you on the inside, and you'll be faithful and true on the outside.

Now allow yourself to think of this as a new adventure, just another opportunity to experience something new. Adventures can be exciting, fun, or scary because you don't know what to expect. It's the element of not knowing what God has waiting in store for us. Don't be so afraid that you turn down an opportunity to serve Him and thus miss out on all the wonderful blessings He has in store for you. Look to God to give you the courage and faith to succeed at every task and purpose for your life.

> *Peace I leave with you, my peace I give to you; not as the world gives do I give to you.*
> *Let not your heart be troubled, neither let it be afraid.*
>
> **(John 14:27 NIV)**

Step XII—It's A New Day

To help guide you through the healing process of divorce, explain your steps to move forward:

How do you want your life to be and begin?

_____

_____

_____

_____

_____

_____

_____

_____

_____

_____

How would you accomplish this?

Plan your goals for the next year

Imagine only good things going forward in your life and have FAITH!

Testimony

A friend once said there are two sides to any story, and somewhere in between is the truth. This is, for me, my truth. This title is true for many women and men in the twenty-first century. One or the other wants out of the marriage. When my spouse first told me he wanted a divorce, I thought he was angry. We had been married for thirteen years. I did not take the situation for granted. I knew he was serious. I just didn't understand the why's of him wanting a divorce.

1. I was not submissive

2. I put the kids ahead of him

3. We were not going the same way financially

It has taken me over three years to come to terms with my marriage ending. If one or the other of us had been abusive physically/emotionally or adulterous, it would have been easier for me to accept. I needed a more valid reason than the ones I was given. I used to call and ask him why (it bordered on harassment). I just could not get past it. You see, it was not my first marriage, but I certainly thought this one would be my last. I was his baby cakes, the apple of his eye. What was I doing that it could not be fixed? My truth: We had issues but we always worked it out.

MY TRUTH: BE SUBMISSIVE

It was explained to me that a submissive wife should always

follow the Bible word for word. God gave man the vision, not the woman. We could discuss anything, but the final decision regardless of what it might have been was his to make. There would be no compromise. "The Bible has no compromise," per my ex. This was very hard for me to accept. My truth—most of the decisions he made were about things he never really completed, and if he did, it was for him not for me.

My Truths:

> 1. He went to college to make things better for us and to secure our future. (He earned his doctorates in Theology.)
>
> 2. The new house was to be our retirement home. (Wanted to lease it out and we move somewhere else. Says he never told me this would be a retirement home.)
>
> 3. Half of all income earned when invited to preach was to be shared equally. (He committed this to me). He stopped giving the half.
>
> 4. Commuting to Oklahoma from Dallas every week to pastor his father's church. (I did not commute every Sunday to Oklahoma because even though the vision was not mine, something in my spirit knew it wouldn't last. He was installed as Pastor, and within six months he resigned. It's his truth to tell as to exactly what happened)

5. Moving to different churches five times, (his decision and I was to follow)

6. Organizing a church (supported this 100%). He disbanded the church. (His truth to tell not mine because I would be lying if I said I understood fully his reasoning for organizing in the first place.) His vision was to organize; my purpose was to be submissive and follow. The final decision was his.

7. Starting a web based business. (I did not help on this, nor did I support it financially.) Nothing else ever worked so why should I believe this would.

8. His vision to write a book. He wrote the book and ended up giving most of them away. (It was a good book.)

By now I know you are wondering what this has to do with submissiveness. MY TRUTH—some of the above issues were discussed with me, and some were not. The final decision was his regardless of what affect it had on me. MY TRUTH—none of them benefitted physically, emotionally, or financially. They were his decisions and the osmosis of "SUBMISSIVENESS."

THE KIDS: My ex was always good to my kids. He always said there were no steps in his house. They were all his kids, and he never wavered from that until the end of the marriage. He has three kids from previous marriages, and I had two kids from a previous marriage. He asked me before we got married this question, and I quote "If we were on a sinking ship who would you save - me or the kids." I said without hesitation "the kids, not just mine but yours too. We have lived our lives, and I want the kids to have the opportunity to live theirs. He said before he married me he would ask me that again, and if I did not change my answer, then we would not marry. He was in no way cruel about this issue but that was HIS TRUTH. I never changed my answer, and we were married. He says a friend explained it to him about a mother's instinct to save the children.

MY TRUTH: If the kids wanted or needed anything from advice to money, I did not always consult him. As a matter of fact on most issues involving "ALL" the kids, I did not consult him. You see my previous spouse (not her father) exposed himself to my daughter when she was nine years old, and I told my ex all about it. I make no excuses for myself other than I was very protective of my daughter. I got counseling, but I always protected her even as an adult. I felt it was my fault that happened, and I let her down. Toward the end of the marriage, my ex had asked me, and then he told me, I needed to stop keeping my six-month-old grandbaby. I had kept her from birth. I kept her during the day, and usually by seven she was gone. During this time my ex had asked me for a divorce, and he had also started to work on his new business venture. He came to me and asked that I not keep the baby in our home anymore because she was disturbing him while he was trying to work. Of course I immediately, without hesitation, said "no." The ultimate [trial?] came when he went to my daughter's house and told her he had asked me for a divorce and he would prefer I come to her house to keep the baby. I found out about this when my daughter's biological father (my ex) called me and told me what happened and asked to speak to my current husband. Needless to say, I was devastated. After he got off the phone, I asked no questions, but I did tell him that he knew the situation with my daughter and asked why would he do that. To me, it was as if the molestation was happening all over again. I did say, and I quote, "To me you are a dead man walking, you are no better than Blank. (Not real name). You just as well have molested her physically because it has the same affect for me." My daughter emailed me the next day, saying again it was her fault that my husband was upset with me. It was then that I realized that this man was serious about wanting out of this marriage. He picked the one thing he knew would send me over the edge and it did.

MY TRUTH: FINANCES: This should have been first, but I saved it for last. When I met my spouse, I had managed my finances for over twenty years, and I will admit they were not in the best of shape but neither were his. He had filed bankruptcy, and that little voice in my head kept saying. *no way*. Eventually after many years and much discussion, I started depositing my check into his account. He did allow me to handle the finances once, but he said I did not send his child support check once, and that was grounds for him to take back the finances. I found the envelope between the seats of my car and showed it to him. I still have the envelope and the check. He took back the finances.

MY TRUTH: I paid my car note, car insurance, bought my own clothes, bought the food, my personal items, and whatever else I needed. When he sold his house, he paid off all my bills before moving to the new house. Keep in mind these are "MY TRUTHS." He paid the house note and utility bills and received on average $1,500 from my pay every two weeks. That's $3,000 a month. We married in 1993. I gave this amount from 1998 until I retired in 2003. I do have documented proof of this. In March of 2004, I gave him $30,000 to pay off all his bills. Not mine, but his. I paid my own off. These are both our "TRUTHS." I have the copies to prove this. I opened a charge account in his name and bought his plane tickets to Oklahoma each week. When he found out about it, he was very upset and I could not blame him. I never missed a payment, and I have documented proof of that. I will admit I was wrong, and I offer no excuses. He came and asked me to file bankruptcy. I disagreed at first because I had no reason to file bankruptcy. I may have had bills but ("MY TRUTH") it was nothing I could not pay. I agreed and filed with him. Once the bankruptcy was settled three weeks to the day, he came to get his things and left.

MY FINAL TRUTH: My divorce was finalized in April of 2005. In October of 2005 my spouse was remarried. I will not lie; I went through all the phases: denial, grief, and anger. I felt so stupid, humiliated, and hurt, all at the same time. I just couldn't understand the why of it all. I was retired and my income was not such that I could afford the house. I kept it because it was my home.

MY TRUTH: I was not being stubborn trying to hold on to a material possession. It was my home, and I wanted to keep it. I don't know what his truth is or was, and I didn't, and still, don't care. This was the first home I ever had that was mine, and I wanted to make a go of keeping it. I was unemployed for over a year. I ended up losing my house and my car.

MY TRUTH: Yes I did, in part, blame my ex. He sat in that office and filled out my retirement papers. I signed on the dotted line. No taxes were taken out of that money, and he says it's my fault.

MY TRUTH: I gave no argument. He had the finance degree. I trusted he knew what he was doing. The S!!! hit the fan when tax time came around. I owed and still owe the IRS $60,000. My ex filed his taxes separate from mine in 2004. He got a refund and kept it all. The rest, as they say, is history.

MY TRUTH: You may be wondering what, if anything, I want you to understand, learn, gain or not gain from my experience. Time, as the saying goes, heals all wounds. Know this—it may not be easy, but you can and will get through it. There are days when I still wonder why he left, and when those moments come, I call upon friends that have been there for me from the beginning. Get a support system of friends who will not be negative. Don't let people tell you anything they heard or saw. What does it matter, he or she is gone. When you feel like calling him/her or wanting to destroy something of theirs, get an old picture and use your imagination. It only hurts you, not them, and it certainly won't make them come back. There are no guarantees in any relationship or marriage; you have to trust that God has put you two together, and no man can turn it asunder.

Divorce Hurts: He Doesn't Want Me as His Wife Anymore

It's funny because my ex told me that, and he really based our marriage on scripture. The main thing is first, FORGIVE YOURSELF and FORGIVE HIM/HER. I called my ex a few times and asked him to forgive me, but I did not mean a word of it. In March of 2009, I called him and I asked him to forgive. I know he thought I was crazy but I really meant it that time. He does let me know in that subtle way of his that he and the new wife are doing fine. He's getting ready to retire, and they are building a home. She lets him make the final decision. You know what? Once I forgave myself and him, life is not a bed of roses for me, yet but I'm getting there. And you will too.

Linda Walters

CONCLUSION

The fact is, divorce hurts and dealing with the hurt and pain is usually very difficult. When you go through the struggles and adversities of the hurt and pain, the devil expects and wants you to give up, become upset, lose your joy, complain, and question God's plan for your life...all those "Why me?" questions. The devil has already devised a plan to destroy your marriage, your family and to keep you in a state of defeat. When you make a conscious choice to obey God's Word and refuse to give up, sin, or get upset, you will release the heavenly forces of the Lord so that the enemy CANNOT take control over your life.

Not only will divorce affect every aspect of your life, but also your children and family. My hope and prayer is that my real life story will provide support and guidance to those going through a similar situation. Realize you are not alone in dealing with the hurt and pain associated with divorce. It is important for you to keep a journal and write out your feelings in order for them not to build up inside you. When you start looking at your past, take it one day at a time, and soon the pain will go way. Pray for those who hurt and spitefully use you to their own benefit. Do not let that old devil influence you into sinful acts. Just obey God's word and rebuke temptation. Surround yourself with positive people who are concerned with your best interest and are not helping the devil defeat you.

Divorce Hurts: He Doesn't Want Me as His Wife Anymore

If you are having trouble in your marriage, be encouraged in the Lord. When the enemy attacks your marriage, children, or family, the enemy would tell you to give up on them, but the Holy Spirit will speak to your heart, and God will stand in the gap and fight for your marriage. Listen to what God is trying to tell you. At times your marriage may get weak spiritually, and it's difficult to fight back. Let the enemy know he's a liar and your marriage belongs to God and let your spouse know as well.

My pastor's wife once gave me a note that stated, "I believe God allows the enemy the first shot at us...God knows the situation better than we do." As my pastor has said many times, Romans 8:28 is so true. The enemy wants to sidetrack you, but take a stand, for the battle is not yours, but God's. (2 Chronicles 20:15) Always praise the Lord, my dear brothers and sisters in Christ! I am still not all I should be, but I am focusing all my energies on this one thing: forgetting the past and looking forward to what lies ahead of me. I strain to reach the end of the race and receive the prize for which God, through Christ Jesus, has prepared for me and who will soon be calling us all up to heaven.

> *Brethren, I do not count myself to have apprehended; but one thing I do, forgetting those things which are behind and reaching forward to those things which are ahead, I press toward the goal for the prize of the upward call of God in Christ Jesus.*
>
> **(Philippians 3: 13-14 NIV)**

FOR MORE INFORMATION

Dana Mobley-Hammett is available for conferences, seminars, and other speaking engagements. She can speak on a variety of topics also related to family, career, education, purpose, relationships, attitude, self-esteem, and personal motivation.

To contact Dana regarding speaking at your event, please email her at:

help@mydivorcehurts.com

Her future project will include writing a sequel to *Divorce Hurts*, on the male view point of "She does not want me to be her husband anymore."

SCRIPTURES FOR HEALING

"Always be joyful. Keep on praying. No matter what happens, always be thankful, for this is God's will for you who belong to Jesus Christ." (1 Thessalonians 5:16-18)

"What is faith? It is the confident assurance that something we want is going to happen. It is the certainty that what we hope for is waiting for us, even though we cannot see it up ahead." (Hebrews 11:1)

"Be good to your servant, that I may live and obey your word. Open my eyes to see the wonderful truths in your instructions." (Psalm 119:17-18)

"The Lord rewards every man for his righteousness and faithfulness." (1 Samuel 26:23)

"Be imitators of God, therefore, as dearly loved children and live a life of love, just as Christ loved us and gave himself up for us as a fragrant offering and sacrifice to God." (Ephesians 5:1-2)

"Be joyful in hope, patient in affliction, and faithful in prayer." (Romans 12:12)

"Do not take revenge, my friends, but leave room for God's wrath for it is written: 'It is mine to avenge; I will repay', says the Lord." (Romans 12:19)

"Am I now trying to win the approval of men, or of God? Or am I trying to please men? If I were still trying to please men, I would not be a servant of Christ." (Galatians 1:10)

"The Lord is my strength and my shield; my heart trusts in him, and I am helped. My heart leaps for joy and I will give thanks to him in song." (Psalm 28:7)

"There is hope in your future." (Jeremiah 31: 17)

ACKNOWLEDGMENTS

I would like to thank my heavenly Father, my Lord and Savior Jesus Christ for allowing me to fulfill this purpose *Divorce Hurts*, and To God Be the Glory!

I would like to thank the women who allowed me to share their testimonies regarding their personal stories on how divorce affected and hurt them.

I would like to thank my loving and supportive children, parents, brothers, sisters, and pastor and wife, each member of my family and special friends. When there was trouble in my life, especially the divorce, and the chips were down, I could depend on all of you, those people that really love me. Thank you for loving me back to health, both mentally and physically.

I would like to thank Dema, a wonderful woman who takes care of my hair. Thanks for being there every step of the way. Thank you for all your encouraging words to continue to let God use me to help other women and men through my story.

I would like to thank Harry for blessing me with your friendship and my photograph.

A special thanks to Yorkshire Publishing, especially Todd and Lily, for your guidance and dedication.

Last but definitely not least, to my wonderful, and supportive husband (Richard) whom I recently married that has given me friendship, honesty, commitment and love. I thank you for your encouragement to continue with God's purpose and write this book to help someone else dealing with divorce.

BIBLIOGRAPHY

Eggerichs, Dr. Emerson, *Love & Respect*, Thomas Nelson, Nashville, Tennessee, 2005.

Kline Carol, Marci Shimoff, *Happy for No Reason*, Free Press, New York, New York, 2008.

Lane, Eddie B., Building *Lasting Family Relationships*, Black Family Press, Dallas, Texas, 1994.

Meyer, Joyce, *The Battle Belongs to the LORD*, Harrison House, Tulsa, Oklahoma, 2002.

Missler, Chuck & Nancy, *Be Ye Transformed; Understanding God's Truth*, The Kings Highway Ministries, Inc., Coeur d' Alene, ID, 1996.

Nee, Watchman, *Spiritual Authority,* Christian Fellowship Publishers, Inc. New York, New York, 1972.

Omartian, Stormie, *The Power of a Praying Wife*, Harvest House Publishers, Eugene, Oregon, 1997.

Roberson, Jerry & Carol, *Strongman's His Name II,* Shiloh Publishing House, Woodburn, Oregon, 1994.

Shire, June & Cheril Huber, *How You Do Anything Is How You Do Everything*, Keep It Simple Books, Unknown, 1998.

Warren, Rick, *The Purpose Driven Life,* Zondervan, Grand Rapids, Michigan, 2002.